Applied Linguistics and Language Study
GENERAL EDITOR: C. N. CANDLIN

Stylistics
and the
Teaching of Literature

H. G. WIDDOWSON

LONGMAN

LONGMAN GROUP UK LIMITED
*Longman House, Burnt Mill, Harlow,
Essex CM20 2JE, England
and Associated Companies throughout
the world.*

First published 1975
Eighth impression 1988

*Produced by Longman Group (FE) Ltd
Printed in Hong Kong*

ISBN 0-582-55076-9

Acknowledgements

I should like to thank Alex Rodger for giving me the benefit of a literary perception much sharper than mine. My thanks are also due to Marillene and Patrick Allen, Mirjana Bonačić, and Mick Short for their comments on an earlier draft of this book.

H. G. W.

We are grateful to the following for permission to reproduce copyright material:

Jonathan Cape Ltd. and Holt, Rinehart and Winston Inc. for the poems 'Dust of Snow', 'Stopping by Woods on a Snowy Evening' and 'After Apple-Picking' from *The Poetry of Robert Frost* edited by Edward Connery Lathem, 1969. Copyright 1923, 1930, 1939, © 1969 by Holt, Rinehart and Winston Inc. Copyright 1951 © 1958 by Robert Frost. Copyright © 1967 by Lesley Frost Ballantine. Reprinted by permission of Holt, Rinehart and Winston Inc. and the Estate of Robert Frost; Author's Agents and Doubleday & Company Inc. for an extract from 'Mackintosh' by W. Somerset Maugham in *The Complete Short Stories of W. Somerset Maugham*. Reprinted by permission of the Estate of W. Somerset Maugham and William Heinemann Ltd.; Faber and Faber Ltd. and Doubleday & Company Inc. for the poem 'Child on Top of a Greenhouse' by Theodore Roethke from *The Collected Poems of Theodore Roethke*. Copyright 1946 by Editorial Publications Inc. Reprinted by permission of Doubleday & Company Inc.; Faber and Faber Ltd. and Harper & Row, Publishers Inc. for the poem 'Wind' from *The Hawk In The Rain* by Ted Hughes. Copyright © 1956 by Ted Hughes. Reprinted by permission of Harper & Row, Publishers Inc.; Faber and Faber Ltd. and New Directions Publishing Corporation for the

poem 'In a Station of the Metro' in *Collected Shorter Poems* by
Ezra Pound. Copyright 1926 by Ezra Pound, Personae. Reprinted
by permission of New Directions Publishing Corporation; Faber
and Faber Ltd. and Oxford University Press Inc. for the poem
'Prayer Before Birth' from *The Collected Poems of Louis MacNeice*,
edited by E. R. Dodds. Copyright © The Estate of Louis MacNeice
1966. Reprinted by permission of Oxford University Press Inc.;
Faber and Faber Ltd. and Random House Inc. for two poems 'Two
Songs for Hedli Anderson' and 'Musée des Beaux Arts' both by
W. H. Auden from *Collected Shorter Poems 1927-1957*. Reprinted by
permission of Faber and Faber Ltd.; Granada Publishing Ltd. and
Harcourt Brace Jovanovich Inc. for two poems 'anyone lived in a
pretty how town' and 'me up at does' by e e cummings from
Complete Poems 1913-1962. Copyright 1940 'anyone lived in a
pretty how town', Copyright 1968 by Marion Morehouse Cummings.
Reprinted by permission of Harcourt Brace Jovanovich Inc. Copy-
right 1963 'me up at does' by Marion Morehouse Cummings.
Reprinted by permission of Harcourt Brace Jovanovich Inc.; Author's
Agents and Macmillan Publishing Company Inc. for a poem 'Leda
and the Swan' and an extract from 'An Irish Airman Foresees His
Death' both by W. B. Yeats from *The Collected Poems of W. B.
Yeats*. Copyright 1928 'Leda and the Swan' by Macmillan Publishing
Company Inc. Renewed 1956 by Georgie Yeats. Copyright 1919 'An
Irish Airman Foresees His Death' by Macmillan Publishing Company
Inc. Renewed 1947 by Bertha Georgie Yeats. Reprinted by permission
of M. B. Yeats, Miss Anne Yeats, Macmillan of London &
Basingstoke and Macmillan Co. of Canada; Author's Agents and
The Viking Press Inc. for two extracts from *The Rainbow* by D. H.
Lawrence and for an extract from 'Fanny & Annie' in *The Collected
Short Stories of D. H. Lawrence*. Reprinted by permission of
Laurence Pollinger Ltd. and the Estate of the late Mrs Frieda
Lawrence.

Preface

Let me try to select some of the reasons why I regard Henry Widdowson's book as making a considerable contribution to extending our view of the principles underlying language teaching and curriculum design, and not only as an expansion of the *Applied Linguistics and Language Study* series to the field of analysing and appreciating literary texts. His concentration on understanding discourse and his view of stylistics as a dynamic way of mediating between linguistics and literary criticism always possesses a wider perspective than mollifying the literary critic's suspicion of linguistic analysis.

Dr Widdowson begins by distinguishing the notion *discipline* from the pedagogic *subject* in order to demonstrate that stylistics is Janus-like in the way it can be treated, for example, at school or university, as a way from linguistics to literary study or the reverse. To understand this bidirectionality he explains distinctions between the linguist's *text* and the critic's *messages* by introducing the concept of *discourse* as a means through which to understand the communicative value of passages of language. Now it is this emphasis on communicative value which is of greatest importance to the development of teaching materials for language learning, whether oriented towards the study of literary texts or not. For too long materials have remained at the surface patterns of linguistic *text*, and have not drawn learners towards an understanding of the layers of meaning which can be peeled off from utterances; learners have seen sentences only as illustrations of grammatical patterns and have not asked pragmatic and sociolinguistic questions of what communicative value they have in given settings.

In discussing this relationship between the grammaticalness of text and the interpretability of discourse, the author does more than to suggest ways in which linguistic elements function to communicative effect. His emphasis on training the student in *interpretative procedures* as a counterweight to 'told' meanings suggests teaching strategies which would have wider application than the treatment of literary texts. How frequently in language teaching textbooks is the chance missed for the student himself to discover rules of language and language use; implicit here is an alternative pedagogic approach to language teaching, well exemplified by the author in his chapter on *Exercises in Literary Understanding*.

Although I have stressed the book's wider importance, it has literary texts as its object of study, and here, particularly in Chapter Four, Dr Widdowson looks at the social context of non-literary messages as a way of highlighting the nature of literary communication as suspended from the accepted sociolinguistic bases of everyday interaction. His detailed investigation of literary texts 'going beyond the limits of the conventionally communicable' serves to make plain the patterning that is possible even where, as in his literary examples, conventional social and grammatical rules are breached.

Finally, one can take the author's tenet that stylistics should develop the individual capacity of response to language use to show how this and the views expressed earlier on the nature of discourse combine to suggest ways of approaching other areas of English language teaching. There is much in common with Dr Widdowson's approach to literary texts in ways of analysing the communicative value of conversations, and, though at first most remote from the examples and thesis of the book, with the understanding of the communicative processes of science central to the teaching of reading comprehension in an ESP framework. Though literary texts have their own rules, understanding authors' messages in technical texts involves similar interpretative techniques and most certainly rests on similar appreciation of the discoursal value of connected language.

Christopher N. Candlin, 1975
General Editor

Contents

Contents

Aims and perspectives

This book might be described as an exercise in applied stylistic analysis. Its principal aim can be stated quite briefly: to present a discussion of an approach to the *study* of literature and a demonstration of its possible relevance to the *teaching* of literature. The approach with which I shall be concerned draws a good deal from linguistics and this discipline will provide the general perspective adopted in the discussion. This does not mean, however, that I shall exclude those considerations of interpretation and artistic effect which are the immediate concern of literary criticism. I do not believe that any approach which does so can be said to be dealing with literature at all in any meaningful sense, and in fact most stylistic analysis, even that which purports to follow a strictly linguistic line, is ultimately based on the kind of intuitions which it is the purpose of literary scholarship to develop. I shall, then, move towards literature from a linguistics direction but expect my approach to converge with that of literary criticism at several points on the way.

The perspective of the discussion in the first part of the book is also of course partly determined by the demonstration in the second part. My purpose is to show the relevance of stylistic analysis to the teaching of literature and not (except incidentally) to the practice of literary criticism as a discipline. I believe that linguistics does have something to contribute to literary criticism, just as literary criticism has something to contribute to linguistics, but it is not my present purpose to explore this area of mutual benefit. Over the past few years there have been a number of angry exchanges between scholars of these different persuasions and they have provided a rather distressing spectacle of mutual misunderstanding and distrust. This controversy has not only done considerable disservice to both disciplines but has also deprived the teacher of literature of an opportunity to develop his own methodology. It is this second consequence with which I shall be concerned in this book. I do not wish to become involved in the controversy about the relevance of stylistics to the *discipline* of literary criticism: my concern is to consider how it can be of relevance to the teaching of literature as a *subject*.

This distinction between a discipline and a subject is, in my view, a crucial one and in a subsequent chapter (Chapter 5) I shall be discussing it in detail in relation to literary studies. Meanwhile the basis of the distinction needs to be made clear. I want to define a discipline as a set of abilities, concepts, ways of thinking, associated with a particular area of human enquiry. Geneticists, biochemists, linguists and literary critics for example all follow certain principles of enquiry which characterise their different disciplines. But students are not geneticists or biochemists or linguists or literary critics: they are in the process of acquiring principles not putting them into practice, and some of them (indeed most of them) will only acquire a certain number of these principles and will never achieve the discipline as such at all. This is even more true of schoolchildren. They do not have disciplines like genetics or biochemistry on their timetables but something called 'science': they do not have linguistics and literary criticism but something called 'English language' and 'English literature'. 'Science', 'English language' and 'English literature' are subjects, not disciplines.* Obviously the higher the educational level the more the subject which is studied approximates to the discipline whose acquisition represents the ultimate academic terminal behaviour of the learner. But the majority of learners will, of course, never reach this point. It is for this reason that the terminal behaviour expected of them cannot be the disciplines to which the subjects they are studying are most closely related.

The point I wish to stress is that subjects must be defined at different educational levels in terms of pedagogic objectives, whereas disciplines are defined in terms of theoretical requirements.† Since some of the pupils at a certain level will go on to a higher level the subject has to be defined in such a way as to provide a basis for development, as a stage in a process. Since some pupils will not be proceeding

---

* 'Physics', 'chemistry' and 'biology' also appear on timetables, of course, but they are pedagogically defined subjects and not simply projections of the disciplines which bear the same names.
† It might be noted that one of the most interesting and difficult problems which arises from this distinction is that explanations which are pedagogically satisfactory in that they make appeal to the pupil's own experience and come within his conceptual range may be unacceptable in terms of the more exact and complex concepts of the disciplines to which the subjects relate.

further in their education, it has also to be defined as a complete process which will fulfil some more general educational purpose. The difficulty in deciding on what constitutes a subject lies primarily in the reconciling of these terminal and non-terminal objectives. This difficulty does not only arise in devising teaching programmes in secondary schools. It arises also (although this may not be very readily acknowledged) in university courses. Very few students go on to do research and to be fully initiated into the discipline of their teachers. A student of literature does not graduate as a literary critic any more than a student of economics graduates as an economist.

It is, then, the relevance of stylistic analysis to literature as a subject that I wish to explore in this book. Of course, since a discipline (or a combination of disciplines) provides the elemental material from which subjects are compounded, what is of relevance to a given subject is likely to have implications for the discipline as well. If the reader wishes to draw out such implications for himself, so much the better but it is not my purpose to dwell on them or to make them explicit.

So much for the aims of this book. The perspectives require a rather more detailed explanation. I have spoken of a linguistic approach and of stylistic analysis and I should make it clear what I intend by these expressions. By 'stylistics' I mean the study of literary discourse from a linguistics orientation and I shall take the view that what distinguishes stylistics from literary criticism on the one hand and linguistics on the other is that it is essentially a means of linking the two and has (as yet at least) no autonomous domain of its own. One can conduct enquiries of a linguistic kind without any reference to literary criticism, and one can conduct enquiries in literary criticism without any reference to linguistics. Some linguists have suggested that the latter is impossible since the literary critic must be involved in a discussion about language. But there are all kinds of ways of talking about language and the linguist's way is only one. The linguist would be first to complain if everyone who talked about language claimed to be talking linguistics. Stylistics, however, involves both literary criticism and linguistics, as its morphological make-up suggests: the 'style' component relating it to the former and the 'istics' component to the latter.

I should add that when I speak of autonomy, I do not wish to imply that linguistics and literary criticism are areas of enquiry which are entirely detached from those of other disciplines: both, for example, have considerable overlap with psychology. But the fact that they draw ideas and techniques from other disciplines does not prevent them from being autonomous. The point I want to make is that, at the present stage of its development, stylistics does not have this status of autonomy, though one might hope that in time it might achieve it.

The view taken in this book, then, is that stylistics is an area of mediation between two disciplines. How far such a mediation is necessary or desirable is, as I have said, a question which I want to keep beyond the scope of this present discussion. What I wish to show is that stylistics can provide a way of mediating between two *subjects*: English language and literature, leaving inexplicit whatever implications arise as to the way it might serve to relate the disciplines from which these subjects derive their content.

We might express the relationships we have been discussing as follows:

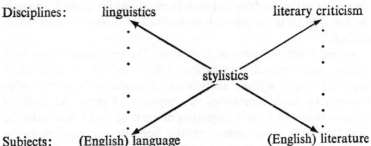

Disciplines: linguistics   literary criticism

stylistics

Subjects: (English) language   (English) literature

This simple diagram seeks to capture the fact that stylistics is neither a discipline nor a subject in its own right, but a means of relating disciplines and subjects. As the diagram indicates, this relationship is not only between discipline and discipline, subject and subject but also between subject and discipline and the reverse. In other words I am making the claim that stylistics can serve as a means whereby literature and language as subjects can by a process of gradual approximation move towards both linguistics and literary criticism, and also a means whereby these disciplines can be pedagogically treated to yield different subjects. Thus stylistics can, I suggest, provide for the progression of a pupil from either language or literature towards either literary criticism or linguistics.

What I understand by stylistics is perhaps now clear enough. Four other terms in the diagram remain undefined. How the two subjects might be defined will be taken up in the second part of the book (in Chapter 5) when I attempt to demonstrate the pedagogic applications of the discussion in the first part. This discussion depends, however, on an understanding of the nature of the two disciplines or, rather, on an understanding of what I conceive their nature to be.

I assume that the ultimate purpose of literary criticism is to interpret and evaluate literary writings as works of art and that the primary concern of the critic is to explicate the individual message of the writer in terms which make its significance clear to others. His task is to decipher a message encoded in an unfamiliar way, to express its meaning in familiar and communal terms and thereby to provide the private message with a public relevance. This activity is not essentially different from that of the critics of other art forms. They decipher non-verbal messages into a verbal form whereas the literary critic deciphers messages from one verbal form into another. Now obviously to do this he must be sensitive to language but his concern is not principally with the way the signals of the artist are constructed but with the underlying message which an interpretation of these signals will reveal. Furthermore, he is less interested in devising a metalanguage into which the original message can be transferred than in conveying the essential significance through exegesis and evaluation and using whatever means of expression seem most appropriate, often drawing on the same kind of figurative and evocative uses of language which characterise the message he is interpreting.

The literary critic, then, is primarily concerned with messages and his interest in codes lies in the meanings they convey in particular instances of use. The linguist, on the other hand, is primarily concerned with the codes themselves and particular messages are of interest in so far as they exemplify how the codes are constructed. Given a piece of literature, a poem for example, the linguist will be interested in finding out how it exemplifies the language system, and if it contains curiosities of usage how these curiosities might be accounted for in grammatical terms. This is not to say that the linguist will necessarily ignore the meanings which the poem conveys and indeed, it may well be the case that the linguist's analysis of the language of a poem is dependent on some prior intuitive interpretation of what the poem is about. But although interpretation may be an aid to his analysis it is not its aim. The literary critic, however, takes interpretation as his aim. He is interested in finding out what aesthetic experience or perception of reality the poem is attempting to convey and his observation of how the language system is used will serve only as a means to this end. The purpose of stylistics is to link the two approaches by extending the linguist's literary intuitions and the critic's linguistic observations and making their relationship explicit.

The linguist, then, directs his attention primarily to how a piece of literature exemplifies the language system. We will say that he treats literature as *text*, and in the following chapter I shall be examining the kind of results which emerge from such a treatment. The literary critic searches for underlying significance, for the essential artistic vision that the poem embodies and we will say that he treats literary works as *messages*. Between these two is an approach to literature which attempts to show specifically how elements of a linguistic text combine to create messages, how, in other words, pieces of literary writing function as a form of communication. Let us say that this approach treats literature as *discourse*. It is this approach (discussed in Chapters 3 and 4) which is most centrally stylistic in the sense in which I have defined that term in the preceding discussion, and which, in my view, promises to have most potential value for the teaching of literature.

I must make one further point about the scope of this book. I have made reference in these introductory remarks both to literature in general and to English literature in particular and I should make it clear that the discussion that follows draws exclusively on literature in the English language as the source of illustration. I assume, however, that a good deal of the discussion has a more general relevance and could, in principle, be illustrated by reference to literature in other languages. Similarly, although my concern is with the teaching of English language and literature, I should like to think that much of what I have to say might have some bearing on the problems of teaching language and literature in general.

Literature as text

Generally speaking, literature has attracted the attention of linguists for two quite opposing reasons. One of them is that it represents data which can be accounted for in terms of models of linguistic description and the other that it represents data which cannot be so accounted for. The first reason is expressed by Halliday as follows:

> Linguistics is not and will never be the whole of literary analysis, and only the literary analyst—not the linguist—can determine the place of linguistics in literary studies. But if a text is to be described at all, then it should be described properly; and this means by the theories and methods developed in linguistics, the subject whose task is precisely to show how language works.*

In Halliday's view (at least, as expressed in the article from which the above quotation is taken) the description of the linguistic elements that occur in a piece of literary writing, the account of how it exemplifies the system of the language, is part of the analysis of the piece of writing as a literary work. In this article, Halliday considers Yeats' poem *Leda and the Swan* and describes how two parts of the system of English are exemplified in it: the first being the nominal group and the second the verbal group. What I want to do now is to consider Halliday's claim by looking at his discussion of the first of these. We will try to establish what contribution his observations make to an understanding of the poem: whether and to what extent they can be regarded as a part of a literary analysis.

LEDA AND THE SWAN

A sudden blow: the great wings beating still
Above the staggering girl, the thighs caressed
By the dark webs, her nape caught in his bill,
He holds her helpless breast upon his breast.

---

* M. A. K. Halliday, 'Descriptive Linguistics in Literary Studies' in Angus McIntosh and M. A. K. Halliday *Patterns of Language: Papers in general, descriptive and applied linguistics*, Longman, 1966, p. 67.

How can those terrified vague fingers push
The feathered glory from her loosening thighs?
And how can body, laid in that white rush,
But feel the strange heart beating where it lies?

A shudder in the loins engenders there
The broken wall, the burning roof and tower
And Agamemnon dead.
                   Being so caught up,
So mastered by the brute blood of the air,
Did she put on knowledge with his power
Before the indifferent beak could let her drop?

As Halliday observes, the definite article in English can function
in a number of different ways and can be distinguished in the grammar
accordingly. In general, its function is to signal that the nominal
group in which it appears constitutes a specific reference. This
reference may be of three kinds. Firstly, it may be contained within
the group itself in the form of a modifier (which precedes the head
word in the group) or of a qualifier (which follows it). Thus, in the
nominal group *the white goddess* the modifier *white* in association
with the definite article specifies a particular goddess. Similarly, *the
goddess in the temple* has definite reference since the qualifier *in the
temple* in association with the definite article again specifies a
particular goddess. Where the definite article signals that some other
element in the nominal group (modifier or qualifier or both) indicates
a specific reference, the article is said to be cataphoric. This might be
expressed as follows:

	M(odifier)	H(ead)	Q(ualifier)
The	white	goddess	
The		goddess	in the temple
The	white	goddess	in the temple

A second kind of reference is one which links the head of the
nominal group with something previously mentioned. If I have been
talking about a goddess, for example, I may say something like 'The
goddess was a figure of great mystery' and here I specify again a
particular goddess, one who had been previously talked about.
Where the definite article signals that the nominal group relates to
what has been referred to before, as in this case, the article is said
to be anaphoric.

A third kind of reference is said to occur when, given a certain
situation, the head word itself is sufficient to identify something
specific and requires no additional elements in the nominal group

nor any link with previous mention to be understood as constituting a specific reference. Such a use of the article is known as homophoric (or exophoric) and examples would be *the sun* or *the moon* where only one referent is possible (assuming that the speaker is not discussing any heavenly body other than earth) and *The Queen*, when this is understood to refer uniquely to the Queen of the United Kingdom and *the President* when this is understood to refer uniquely to the President of the United States.

It will be noticed that in this account of the definite article two quite different kinds of criteria have been used. On the one hand, appeal has been made to the way the nominal group is structured, so that one can say: if the nominal group has either a modifier or a qualifier or both, then the definite article is cataphoric and if not it is either anaphoric or homophoric. On the other hand, appeal has been made as to how the nominal group functions as communication, so that one can say: if the nominal group itself constitutes a specific reference and does not depend on being linked to anything else then the definite article is cataphoric. The first kind of criteria has to do with linguistic form and the second with communicative function, and the relationship between them is of considerable importance in this particular poem, as we shall see.

Halliday notices that in *Leda and the Swan* there are 25 nominal groups (excluding those consisting only of pronouns and the name *Agamemnon*) of which 10 contain the definite article with either a modifier or a qualifier or both. This information is set down in the form of a table. What we have so far is a simple example of text analysis. But now a complication arises: although by formal criteria the definite articles in these 10 nominal groups must be counted as cataphoric, they do not seem to operate as such if one takes functional criteria into account. That is to say, these nominal groups do not seem to make the kind of self-contained reference which Halliday suggests characterises the cataphoric use of the article. For example, the expressions *the great wings beating still* and *the dark webs* meet the formal conditions for cataphora (their structure as nominal groups being MHQ, and MH respectively) but the wings are not identified as kinds of wings which are great and beating, nor the webs as kinds of webs which are dark. Rather the reference appears to be to something outside the nominal group and therefore, with respect to function, to be either anaphoric or homophoric in Halliday's terms.

Halliday himself notices this discrepancy between the form of these nominal groups and the function they appear to have in the poem. The dark webs, the great wings and the staggering girl are, he says, identified anaphorically by reference to the title of the poem, so that the dark webs and the great wings relate to the swan and the staggering girl to Leda. He then adds:

> The only other type of writing I can call to mind in which this feature is found at such a high density is in tourist guides and, sometimes, exhibition catalogues. (I hope I need not add that this is in no sense intended as an adverse criticism of the poem.)*

Now clearly the way in which the poem as text exemplifies different nominal group structures is, as isolated information, of very slight interest and this aspect of Halliday's analysis, on its own, cannot be said to contribute anything to an understanding of the poem as such. What is of interest is that these groups do not appear to function as they most commonly do but in a way which is found in certain restricted uses of English. We may take the point that the comparison between *Leda and the Swan* with an exhibition catalogue is not intended as an adverse criticism but it does imply criticism in the sense in which literary critics use that term. Halliday begins with text analysis and shows how a part of the language system is exemplified in the poem. He then points to the fact that this part of the system is being *used* in a somewhat unusual way. This prepares the ground for a discussion of the poem as discourse, that is to say for a consideration of how these linguistic facts are relevant to an understanding of the message which the poem conveys. But having come to this stylistic brink, Halliday withdraws with a final provocative remark. His primary interest lies in the text and the nature of the poem's message is outside his concern.

Let us now attempt, briefly, to extend Halliday's observations into a stylistic analysis in the sense defined in Chapter 1 by considering the use of these nominal groups as features of the poem as a discourse. If their use of forms which are commonly 'cataphoric' is in fact 'anaphoric' in the manner of exhibition catalogues and tourist brochures what does this tell us about the meaning of the poem?

We will begin by a brief consideration of how anaphoric reference works. A nominal group can be linked up with one preceding if some kind of semantic association can be made between them. Thus, as Halliday suggests, *the staggering girl* can be linked up anaphorically with *Leda* in the title of the poem since part of the meaning of the

* Halliday, *op. cit.*, p. 59.

name is that it is feminine, or (to put it slightly more technically) the name has a semantic feature /+female/ and this feature is shared by the item *girl*. Similarly *wings* and *webs* being actually bodily parts of birds can be associated with *the swan* in the title. But not all of the nominal groups can be linked with the title so obviously. There is no direct semantic relation, for example, between either Leda or the swan and *The broken wall* or *the burning roof and tower* although it seems evident that neither is cataphoric in function either. There appear to be two possibilities. The first is that the reference here is homophoric: mention of Leda and her encounter with the swan creates a kind of situation in the mind in which broken walls and burning towers must have exclusive reference to Troy, just as being, let us say, in Canterbury creates an actual situation in which any mention without modification or qualification of *the Cathedral* would quite unambiguously refer to Canterbury cathedral. The second possibility is that the reference is in a way homophoric but in a more exact sense than that in which Halliday appears to use the term in that it indicates details in a picture, real or realistically imagined, of which the poem is in fact a direct description. That is to say, the nominal groups here may be functioning *deictically* to point to things supposed to be actually present in the immediate context of utterance.

Let us explore this second possibility a little further. If it is the case that the high incidence of nominal groups usually cataphoric but functioning in a non-cataphoric way is a feature of the way English is used in tourist guides and exhibition catalogues, then it is pertinent to ask why they are so used. The answer would seem to be that it is because the nominal groups are deictic in function, making reference to external objects which it is assumed will be present to the reader when he reads and thus part of the situation: paintings or sculptures, churches or castles or other ancient buildings. Consider, for example, the following extract from a guide to Florence:

> The graceful Loggia in the Florentine Gothic style with round arches was the place to which unwanted children were taken. The three statues in the tabernacles on the font represent the *Madonna and Child between St. Lucy and St. Peter Martyr*. They are of the Pisan school of the 14th Century. The frescoes which once adorned the façade were removed to save them from the inclemencies of the weather. . . .

The nominal groups which serve as subjects in the first two of these sentences are similar to those in the Yeats' poem we have been discussing in that although their structure would seem to indicate that the definite article is cataphoric they in fact function deictically since the nominal groups relate to what it is assumed the visitor will see as he walks around, guide-book in hand. The same would be true if these sentences referred to maps or photographs in the guide-book itself. Thus these sentences have a communicative function which we might make explicit in the following manner: 'The graceful Loggia, *which you see before you on the left of the altar* . . .' 'The three statues, *illustrated below* . . .' The last sentence in the extract provides an interesting comparison with the first two for here the reference *is* cataphoric in function: the frescoes cannot become part of the situation in which the tourist finds himself because they are no longer there. They are identified independently by the nominal group itself.

If the nominal groups in *Leda and the Swan* are deictic in the same way as those in the tourist guide-book we have just been considering then it suggests that Yeats is describing either an actual picture or one which is clearly delineated in his mind as a precise vision. Furthermore the picture, real or imagined, includes the broken wall and the burning towers of Troy. That Yeats is describing from a definite 'model'—defined clearly in reality or in his mind—rather than simply associating ideas, as it were, is suggested by two further observations. The first is the use of the definite article in the nominal group *the thighs caressed by the dark webs*. This follows the group *the staggering girl* which could relate to the title. But since this latter group establishes the link with Leda identifying her as the girl, there seems no motivation for using the definite article in the one which follows: we would expect *her thighs* . . . The use of the definite article suggests that *the thighs* relate directly to some detail in a picture rather than to Leda as a referent. The second observation concerns the nominal group *those terrified vague fingers*. Now this demonstrative adjective *those* (as the term 'demonstrative' suggests) has a very definite indicating function. When it is used anaphorically it requires a fairly specific previous mention. But there is nothing very specific in the poem to relate this nominal group with: *those fingers*—but which fingers where? There is nothing in the first verse of the poem that provides a strong enough semantic link to make the use of *those* appropriate, as opposed to *her* or *the*. If we suppose that there is a picture present to the poet, however, and that *those* is being used deictically to point out some detail, then there is no difficulty.

What I am suggesting is that having observed in the poem the incidence of particular kinds of nominal group and noticed a certain peculiarity of use, one can then go on to draw out certain possible implications about the kind of message expressed in the poem. On the evidence of the nominal groups we have considered we can suggest that Yeats is representing his poem as a description of a picture.

He may not have composed the poem with an actual picture in front of him but there is evidence to suggest that he means the picture to be, as it were, 'given' as a necessary complement.* Some kind of support is given to this suggestion by considering the following lines of Auden where the nominal groups function in the same deictic way (even where they contain the usually cataphoric modifier and qualifier elements) as those in *Leda and the Swan*:

> In Brugel's *Icarus*, for instance: how everything turns away
> Quite leisurely from the disaster; the ploughman may
> Have heard the splash, the forsaken cry,
> But for him it was not an important failure; the sun shone
> As it had to on the white legs disappearing into the green
> Water; and the expensive delicate ship that must have seen
> Something amazing, a boy falling out of the sky,
> Had somewhere to get to and sailed calmly on.
>
> (*Musée des Beaux Arts*)

Of course, having suggested that Yeats uses nominal groups in a certain way to achieve the immediacy of direct reference to an exact picture we still have a long way to go before we arrive at an interpretation of the poem as a complete unit of discourse. We have only looked at one linguistic feature of the text and we have advanced a hypothesis as to its significance. But this hypothesis may turn out to be contrary to the evidence offered by other linguistic features, or it may turn out that whether Yeats is directly describing or drawing on an association of ideas is a point which is not significant for the understanding of the poem's message as a whole.

We may say that the description of a poem, or any other piece of literature, as a text, using (as Halliday puts it) 'the theories and methods developed in linguistics' may be a 'proper' one in the sense that it is an accurate specification of how linguistic elements are

---

* Alex Rodger has drawn my attention to the following comment on the poem by Jeffares: 'The source is probably Michelangelo's famous picture at Venice of which Yeats had a coloured photographic copy.' A. Norman Jeffares, *Poems of W. B. Yeats, selected with an introduction and notes*, Macmillan, 1966, p. 120.

exemplified but it does not, on its own, lead to interpretation. It may be regarded as part of literary criticism only if the significance of its findings are investigated and hypotheses are made as to what they contribute to an understanding of the literary work as a discourse. Text analysis provides us, as we have seen, with a way of getting into a poem: it can serve as a very effective means of initial assault. But it does not give a proper description of the poem: it gives a proper description of the linguistic features of the text.

Let us now consider the second reason why literary works have attracted the interest of linguists—that they represent data which *cannot* be accounted for satisfactorily by 'the theories and methods developed in linguistics'. It is this reason which has particularly provoked the interest of linguists working with transformational-generative models of linguistic description. According to linguists of this school the grammar of a language is a device for generating all and only the sentences of that language. Furthermore, the grammar is meant to represent the native speaker's linguistic knowledge and so to account for his ability to produce and interpret his language correctly. It would seem to follow from this that any sentence that is not generated by the grammar is in principle not part of the speaker's knowledge and will therefore if produced not be interpretable. Thus, if I come out with a 'sentence' like:

> You in through into an oven did a rabbit look

it is fair to say that my interlocutor will take it as gibberish. He may have a shot at understanding what I mean if he thinks that I intend to mean something and not just to produce a random string of words, but he will not be able to impose an interpretation on the sentence by virtue of his knowledge of English grammar. The sentence is not a sentence of English and will therefore not be generated by a grammar of English.

In literary writing, however, one constantly comes across sentences which would not be generated by an English grammar but which are nevertheless interpretable. Consider the extreme case of e e cummings. The first lines of the following poem have the same structure (or lack of it) as the string of words above which we have rejected as an unintelligible non-sentence of English, and yet they are interpretable.*

---

* Chomsky himself points this out (*Aspects of the Theory of Syntax*, M.I.T. Press, 1965, p. 228).

Me up at does
out of the floor
quietly Stare
a poisoned mouse

still who alive
is asking What
have i done that
You wouldn't have

This phenomenon of actually attested and interpretable sentences which cannot be generated by the grammar has occupied the attention of a number of linguists. Since such sentences are interpretable, then it might seem reasonable to suppose that the grammar should in principle be able to generate them because the grammar is a model of the speaker's knowledge of his language by virtue of which he is able to interpret the sentences. Since the grammar does not generate them, the question arises as to whether one might adapt it in some way so that it does.

The work of e e cummings has been much discussed in this connection because of its obvious oddity but the problem and the possibility of its solution can be illustrated by reference to literature which shows a less extreme deviance from grammatical rules (and which the literary critic might perhaps regard as more worthy of attention). Consider first the following well-known lines from Shakespeare's *Antony and Cleopatra:*

> . . . and I shall see
> Some squeaking Cleopatra boy my greatness
> I' the posture of a whore   (V. 2)

Now one of the basic sets of distinctions within a grammar is that which distinguishes between different parts of speech, and *boy* would, of course, be specified as a noun in a standard description of English. Here, however, it operates as a transitive verb. Shakespeare is consequently guilty of violating a grammatical rule. But if we wish the grammar to account for the fact that these lines are perfectly intelligible we will have to alter the specification of *boy* so that a sentence which uses it as a transitive verb will be generated. If we do that, however, we must accept that the grammar will now generate a whole host of other sentences in which *boy* functions as a transitive verb: sentences perhaps like:

> Ethel was boying her hair in the bathroom.
> Maggie has boyed her dolls again.

These sentences are not attested as having actually been used, nor is their use here motivated by any artistic purpose, and in this respect we do not want our grammar to generate them. If they were uttered by a child or a foreign learner they would be regarded as incorrect. Here incidentally we touch upon the question of the value of literature as a model of good writing: a question which will be considered in the second part of the book.

For the moment the point to notice is that in literary writing it is common to find instances of language use which cannot be accounted for by grammatical rules. In the case of the lines from Shakespeare quoted above the linguist can note that they constitute a deviant sentence and can specify where the deviance lies: the poet has violated a 'category rule' by transferring the lexical item *boy* from the category of noun to the category of verb and more precisely to the sub-category of transitive verb. This statement is about these lines as text.

The category of verb is sub-categorised into transitive and intransitive. That is to say, there is a 'sub-categorisation' rule in English grammar which distinguishes between the two classes of verb and specifies that a transitive verb is followed by a noun phrase (NP) or (to use Halliday's term) a nominal group, whereas an intransitive verb is not. In the light of these simple grammatical rules consider now the following lines from Ted Hughes' poem *Wind:*

> At noon I scaled along the house-side as far as
> The coal-house door.

Treating these lines as text, we may say that here we have a deviant sentence in that there is a violation of a verb sub-categorisation rule: the verb 'scale' belongs to a class of transitive verbs in modern English but it is treated here as an intransitive one (like 'clamber') or as one which appears in both sub-categories (like 'climb').

Later in the same poem we find the lines:

> We watch the fire blazing,
> And feel the roots of the house move, but sit on,
> Seeing the window tremble to come in.

Apart from a sub-categorisation of verbs in respect of transitivity the grammar also specifies further sub-categories among which would be one of verbs which are followed by to+infinitive. Except in certain phrases (as in 'I tremble to think . . .') the verb 'tremble' is not one of these, and yet in these lines it operates as if it were. To put the matter simply, phrases like 'ask to come in', 'try to come

in', 'hesitate to come in' are normal because they conform to grammatical rules, but 'tremble to come in' is odd because it does not, and
the linguist can specify just which grammatical rule is being violated.

Again, what value for literary interpretation does such a specification have? I will come to that question in a moment. Meanwhile
let us notice that the idea of the window trembling is curious in this
particular context. There is nothing at all odd about windows
trembling in the ordinary way: they do when traffic passes or when
the door slams. But because of the recategorisation which has been
mentioned the verb 'tremble' is associated with verbs which belong
to the sub-category of those which take the to + infinitive like 'try',
'attempt', 'hesitate', 'want' and so on and these normally require
an animate subject. If the line had read: *Seeing the window tremble*
there would be no oddity at all, but the addition of the to + infinitive
to come in both recategorises the verb and, in consequence, bestows
animacy on the subject noun phrase.

Here we come to another kind of rule violation, and one which
is extremely common in literary writing (it is, indeed, common in
many uses of language). Somewhere in a description of English
(though in what part of it is a somewhat controversial matter) there
will be rules which specify that certain verbs require their subjects
or objects or both to contain nouns of a particular kind. For example,
the verb 'see' requires that its subject contain a noun which is animate,
the verb 'hurt' requires that an animate noun operates in the object
and the verb 'assault' requires animacy in both subject and object.
To put the matter more technically there are certain 'selection
restriction rules' or 'collocation rules' in the language description
which prevent the generation of such sentences as the following:

> The thistle saw the gardener.
> The gardener hurt the thistle.
> The thistle assaulted the cauliflower.

but would ensure the generation of sentences like:

> The gardener saw the thistle.
> The thistle hurt the gardener.
> The gardener assaulted the housemaid.

The oddity of the phrase *Seeing the window tremble to come in*
can be accounted for, then, by invoking selection restriction rules
which state that the verb 'tremble' when denoting an animate state
(as it has to in association with *come in* in this context) requires an

animate noun in its subject. This kind of deviance, arising from a violation of selection restriction or collocation rules, is, of course, extremely common in literature. The following are a few random examples:

> The rain set early in tonight,
> The sullen wind was soon awake,
> It tore the elm-tops down for spite,
> And did its best to vex the lake. (Browning)

> The yellow fog that rubs its back upon the window panes,
> The yellow smoke that rubs its muzzle on the window panes.
> (Eliot)*

> The southwest-wind and the west-wind sing (Swinburne)

> There was a whispering in my hearth,
> A sigh of the coal,
> Grown wistful of a former earth
> It might recall. (Owen)

A large number of selection restriction violations involve giving the feature of animacy (or /+animate/) to nouns which are specified as inanimate (or /−animate/) in the description of the language system. Most common of all are instances of inanimate nouns being given not only the feature /+animate/ but also the feature /+human/ as in all the examples cited above except the lines from Eliot.

But the bestowing of animate and human features on normally inanimate nouns is not the only form of deviance from selection restriction rules. Consider for example these lines from Auden's *Two Songs for Hedli Anderson:*

> The stars are not wanted now; put out every one:
> Pack up the moon and dismantle the sun;
> Pour away the ocean and sweep up the woods:
> For nothing now can ever come to any good.

Here the moon and the sun take on a feature like /+artefact/ since the verbs 'pack up' and 'dismantle' require nouns with this feature in their objects. But this is not the only feature required: not all artefacts can be packed up or dismantled. We need to specify other features. But in many cases it is extremely difficult to establish just what features a verb requires its subject or object to have. What features does a noun have to have, for example, before it can correctly operate in an object of the phrasal verbs 'pour away' and 'sweep up'

---

* T. S. Eliot, *Collected Poems 1909-35*, (The Love Song of J. Alfred Prufrock). Faber and Faber, 1936.

in the third of the lines quoted from Auden above? These two verbs would seem to be similar to the two we have just considered in that all of them require a feature in the object noun which we might express roughly as /+human product/ or /+result of human processing/. But we clearly need something more precise than this in a linguistic rule.

Similar difficulties arise in considering the opening lines of Ted Hughes' poem *Wind* which was referred to earlier:

> This house has been far out at sea all night,
> The woods crashing through darkness, the booming hills,
> Winds stampeding the fields under the window . . .

The verb 'stampede', as specified in the language code, may be either transitive or intransitive. When it is intransitive, it requires, in accordance with selection restriction rules, that its subject noun should contain the feature of animacy. When it functions transitively it requires the object noun to have this feature and those nouns which are appropriate as objects of 'stampede' in transitive structures are precisely those which are appropriate as subjects of this verb in intransitive structures. We must note, however, that animacy is not the only feature required of these nouns. A further requirement is that they should refer to a number of animate beings (a stampede is generally associated with a herd or a crowd) and perhaps more specifically to mammals (since neither birds nor fish nor insects are normally said to stampede). The number of necessary features begins to proliferate as we try to single out those which will ensure that a semantically non-deviant sentence will be generated. It is necessary to attempt this, however, because at least some of these features are associated with *fields* in the poem and understanding the normal selection restrictions on the use of 'stampede' will indicate what meaning the poet is trying to convey. I will be considering the pedagogic implications of this point in the second part of the book.

Although it is often very difficult to establish selection restrictions in a precise way, it is on the other hand sometimes extremely easy. This is the case where the verb requires a very specific subject or object noun. Consider, for example, the following line from Rossetti:

> That eve was clenched for a boding storm.
>
> *(The King's Tragedy)*

The object noun for the verb 'clench' in the active voice (and the subject noun in the passive, as in this line) can only be either 'hand', 'fingers', 'fist' or 'teeth' since only the hand or the fingers or the teeth (in the plural) can be clenched in the normal way and then, of course, only by their owner (you cannot clench somebody else's fist or somebody else's teeth).

Here, then, the selection restriction rule can be specified exactly by reference to four lexical items, three of which are semantically related.

So far we have been looking at cases of deviation which can be described as violations of underlying or base rules of grammar. The generative grammarians make a fundamental distinction between two levels of linguistic analysis: the deep and the surface. It is not necessary for the purposes of this book to enter into a detailed discussion of what is involved in such an analysis but the main principles can be stated quite simply. It is easy to think of a number of sentences in English which are equivalent in meaning in the sense that the basic relationship between the semantic elements in each sentence is the same. The most obvious (and most commonly cited) example of such an equivalence is that which holds between active and passive sentences. Thus the sentence:

The expensive coat attracted my wife's attention.

can be said to be equivalent to:

My wife's attention was attracted by the expensive coat.

The generative grammarian would say that these two sentences have the same underlying structure but different surface structures. The underlying structure is described in terms of base rules and then further rules, called transformational rules, are applied to 'generate' the different surface forms. The base rules, then, account for the underlying meaning in virtue of which the two sentences are synonymous. It can be argued, of course, that the two sentences are not synonymous in that the first is about the expensive coat and the second about the attention it attracted and they would not, therefore, be interchangeable in context. This is true, but the relationship between the semantic elements remains the same nevertheless—it is the coat that is doing the attracting and the attention that is being attracted in both cases—so it seems reasonable to say that the two sentences are 'cognitively' synonymous, even though one can accept that they are not in free variation. We may say that cognitive meaning resides in the underlying structure of sentences and transformational rules do not change it.

In this view of linguistic structure, then, active and passive sentences derive from the same deep structure source. The same applies to relative clauses and preposed or attributive adjectives. That is to say, the following sentence would also be derived from the same deep structure as the ones cited above:

The coat which was expensive attracted my wife's attention.

Let us say that the deep structure which underlies these sentences can be roughly paraphrased like this:

The coat/the coat was expensive/attracted my wife's attention.

A transformational rule can now be applied to delete the second occurrence of the noun phrase in the 'embedded' sentence *the coat* and replace it with a relative pronoun. This operation yields one possible surface structure:

The coat which was expensive attracted my wife's attention.

Alternatively, further transformational rules can be applied: by applying one the relative pronoun and the auxiliary are deleted and by applying another the remnant of the relative clause is then transposed to become a preposed adjective:

The coat which was expensive→the coat expensive→
                                    the expensive coat.*

Now if the first of these transformations leaves a remnant which consists of a single lexical item, as is the case here, then the second rule has to be applied. If it were not applied, the following incorrect sentence would be generated:

The coat expensive attracted my wife's attention.

Conversely, if the first transformation were to leave a remnant which consisted of a prepositional phrase, then the second transformation could not be applied. Let us suppose, for example, that we had a deep structure roughly paraphrasable as:

The coat/the coat was in the window/attracted my wife's attention.

---

* In fact the phrase 'The expensive coat' is ambiguous so the sentence is an example of a surface form having two possible deep structures, the other having the alternative surface form: 'The coat, which was expensive, attracted my wife's attention.' For the purpose of the present discussion, however, we can ignore this other possibility.

We can apply a transformational rule to replace the second occurrence of *the coat* with the relative pronoun, as before, and this would yield the possible surface form:

The coat which was in the window attracted my wife's attention.

But, again as before, we might alternatively apply another transformational rule which deletes the relative pronoun and the auxiliary and this will give us another possible surface structure:

The coat in the window attracted my wife's attention.

What we cannot do, however, is to apply a transposing transformation to move the remnant of the relative and place it in front of the noun because we then get the ungrammatical sentence:

The in the window coat attracted my wife's attention.

To put the matter simply, then, if a transformational operation on an embedded sentence leaves a remnant which is a single lexical item, then a further transformational rule must normally be applied to move that remnant to a position in front of the noun. If the remnant is not a single lexical item but a prepositional phrase or other complex structure, then this further transformation must normally *not* be applied.

Let us now return to literature. It is very common to find the conditions for the applicability of these transformations ignored in poetry. Consider, for example, the following lines:

Sometimes a troop of damsels glad,
An abbot on an ambling pad,
Sometimes a curly shepherd-lad,
Or long-haired page in crimson clad,
  Goes by to tower'd Camelot:
And sometimes thro' the mirror blue
The knights come riding two and two:
She hath no loyal knight and true,
  The Lady of Shalott.   (Tennyson)

We can describe the abnormality of *damsels glad* and *the mirror blue* by referring to the transformational processes we have just discussed. The poet has neglected to apply the obligatory rule which transposes the single lexical item remaining after deletion to a position in front of the noun. The fourth line of this extract can also be described by reference to transformational rules, but here the poet has made use of a rule that is not operative in modern English. Let us say that underlying the phrase *a page in crimson clad* is a deep structure of something like the following form:

A page/a page is clad in crimson/

Replacement of the noun phrase in the embedded sentence with a relative pronoun yields:

A page who is clad in crimson.

Deletion of the relative pronoun and the auxiliary gives us:

A page clad in crimson.

So far all is well. But now Tennyson applies a further transformational rule which does not exist in modern English: he transposes the prepositional phrase *in crimson* to a position in front of the verb.

We can see that by invoking certain transformational rules we can describe fairly precisely what the poet is doing to the language and in what respect the text is deviant. What we cannot do simply by describing such linguistic properties is to say why he is manipulating the language in this way. We might suggest that Tennyson does so in this case in order to create an atmosphere of antiquity and romance since the rules he is using are of an archaic and 'poetic' kind, so that the language and the theme are blended together. But to suggest this is to go beyond the text and to consider the nature of the poem as discourse and to go beyond linguistic description towards literary judgement.

The phrases *damsels glad* and *mirror blue* are the outcome of not applying rules which in normal circumstances ought to be applied. We also get instances where rules are applied when the conditions are not appropriate for their application. Hopkins is a poet who is particularly prone to transposing phrasal remnants of embedded sentences instead of leaving them where they ought to be. To take one simple example, consider the phrase *dappled-with-damson west*, which occurs in *The Wreck of the Deutschland*. We can postulate a deep structure for this phrase of roughly the following form:

The west/the west is dappled with damson/

Let us compare this with the underlying structure of the phrase 'The golden west', which would read as follows:

The west/the west is golden/

c

In both cases we can apply the transformational rule which yields a relative clause:

> The west which is dappled with damson.
> The west which is golden.

Alternatively, as before, we can delete the relative pronoun and the auxiliary and this transformation will generate:

> The west dappled with damson
> The west golden

Now, as we have seen, it is necessary to apply a transformational rule to transpose *golden* in the second phrase, but this rule cannot normally apply to the first phrase because the conditions for its application do not obtain. But Hopkins does in fact apply it.

I have said that if the remnant of the embedded sentence is a prepositional phrase then the transposing transformation does not apply. This example from Hopkins makes it clear that there are also other conditions that constrain the application of this rule, and that it is not only the prepositional phrase remnant which prevents the operation taking place. It should also be added that there are remnants consisting of more than a single lexical item which *can* be transposed: returning briefly to Tennyson's lines, for example, consider the phrase *no loyal knight and true*. The stages whereby this phrase is generated can be expressed as follows:

> No knight/the knight is loyal and true/
> No knight who is loyal and true
> No knight loyal and true
> No loyal and true knight.

In this case the last two phrases are normal and it is clear that the existence of a conjoined predicate of this kind constitutes a condition whereby the transposing transformation is optional: one can apply it or not and the result is still a grammatical phrase. What is not normally permissible, however, is to apply a transformational rule which splits up the predicate remnant and transposes only part of it, as Tennyson does.

It is not necessary for the purposes of the present discussion to go into details about the different sets of conditions which are required for a particular transformational rule to be correctly applied. The relevant point is that certain peculiarities of literary texts can be described in fairly exact terms by reference to grammatical rules of this transformational kind. Whether and to what extent such a description is relevant to an understanding of a text as a literary work is a matter which will be taken up later. For the present it has to be pointed out that, as with the case of Halliday's analysis, the description on its own is only of linguistic interest: its significance for literary criticism has to be demonstrated.

Let us review, briefly, the points that have been raised regarding the treatment of literary writing as a kind of text which cannot be accounted for by a standard linguistic description. It is common to find sentences in literature which will not be generated by grammatical rules. It is possible to specify the nature of the deviation of these sentences by referring to the base rules of deep structure, like category rules, sub-categorisation rules and selection restriction rules, and to the transformational rules which derive different surface structures from a single base. The description of English 'along transformational generative lines has not (yet) reached a stage whereby one can state exactly the degree of deviation in a particular instance (this is particularly true with regard to selection restriction rules) and indeed it is often only when one considers deviant sentences such as occur in literature that the extent of the problem becomes apparent. This is one difficulty in applying a linguistic description to the analysis of literary texts. Another difficulty, as has already been pointed out, lies in the relationship between grammaticalness and interpretability. If, as the generative grammarians claim, a grammar is a model of the speaker's knowledge of his language, how does it come about that sentences which are ungrammatical are nevertheless interpretable in the context of a piece of literary writing?

With this second question we arrive at a point of similarity between Halliday's treatment of literary texts and that of the generative grammarians. As we have seen, they start from opposing points of view: Halliday's belief is that literary texts can be accounted for in terms of a standard linguistic description whereas the point that the generative grammarians make is that they very often cannot. In both cases, however, the interest is in literature as textual data, and in both cases we run up against the question: how does the textual analysis relate to the interpretation of a particular literary work as a piece of communication? How does the literary writer's use or misuse of grammatical rules create a particular kind of discourse which we recognise as literature? How does it come about that we understand ungrammatical sentences and what kind of understanding is it that we have? These questions centre on the relationship between the grammaticalness of text and the interpretability of discourse. The investigation of this relationship is taken up in the next chapter.

3

Literature as discourse

In the previous chapter I pointed out a number of ways in which the linguist can describe how literary texts exemplify the system of English as represented in his grammar, or if they do not exemplify it in what respects they deviate from the rules. But a piece of language use, literary or otherwise, is not only an exemplification of linguistic categories—that is to say it is not only text in the sense in which I have defined that term—but is also a piece of communication, a discourse of one kind or another. The question arises then as to what significance textual features have for an understanding of literature as discourse.

Central to this issue is the problem of the relationship between grammaticalness and interpretability which was raised, but left unresolved, in the previous chapter. A grammar purports to represent a speaker's knowledge of his language so that what is ungrammatical should in principle make no sense. But ungrammatical sentences in literary writing do make sense and a poem which deviates from grammatical rules as text is nevertheless interpretable as discourse. How can we explain this fact?

The first point to notice is the obvious one that linguistic deviations do not occur randomly in a literary work but pattern in with other linguistic features, both regular and irregular, to form a whole. They are understood, therefore, not in isolation with reference only to the linguistic system, or code, but also with reference to the context in which they appear. We can show this quite simply by considering the context of one of the quotations we have already cited. We have shown how lines from Ted Hughes' poem *Wind* violate certain grammatical rules: let us now look at the poem as a whole:

WIND

This house has been far out at sea all night,
The woods crashing through darkness, the booming hills,
Winds stampeding the fields under the window
Floundering black astride and blinding wet

27

Till day rose; then under an orange sky
The hills had new places, and wind wielded
Blade-light, luminous and emerald,
Flexing like the lens of a mad eye.

At noon I scaled along the house-side as far as
The coal-house door. I dared once to look up—
Through the brunt wind that dented the balls of my eyes
The tent of the hills drummed and strained its guyrope,

The fields quivering, the skyline a grimace,
At any second to bang and vanish with a flap:
The wind flung a magpie away and a black-
Back gull bent like an iron bar slowly. The house

Rang like some fine green goblet in the note
That any second would shatter it. Now deep
In chairs, in front of the great fire, we grip
Our hearts and cannot entertain book, thought,

Or each other. We watch the fire blazing,
And feel the roots of the house move, but sit on,
Seeing the window tremble to come in,
Hearing the stones cry out under the horizons.

It will be recalled that we had some difficulty in specifying just
what semantic features the verb 'stampede' requires of a noun which
functions as subject in an intransitive sentence and as object in a
transitive one. It might also have been pointed out that the same
kind of problem arises in attempting to specify the required features
of the noun which functions in the subject of a transitive sentence
using 'stampede'. When we consider the phrase *Winds stampeding
the fields* in the context of the poem however, it becomes plain that
such a detailed specification is not necessary since the way this
phrase is conditioned by others in the poem renders many of the
features we might isolate as of little significance. The phrase is
understood partly in terms of itself but partly also in terms of its
relationship with other expressions in the poem in which the words
'wind' and 'fields' occur. These are: (*Wind*) *floundering black astride
and blinding wet, Wind wielded blade-light, The brunt wind that
dented the balls of my eyes, The wind flung a magpie away, The fields
quivering* . . . By relating these different references we get a composite
impression of animate force and violence embodied in the wind
terrorising the panic-stricken fields trembling in animate fear. Of all
the possible features of the nouns which we might specify to ensure
the correct operation of selection restriction rules, what is brought
into prominence here is animacy with the additional feature of

violence and savagery associated with 'wind' and of timidity associated with 'fields'. These are the features which the context brings into focus, leaving others to recede into the penumbra of lesser significance.

It does not seem to be a very fruitful question, then, to ask how *The winds (were) stampeding the fields* is to be interpreted as an isolated sentence, since we are not called upon to interpret it as a sentence but only as a part of the poem as a whole. Within the poem the lexical item *wind* consistently has features which we might express roughly as /+animate/ and /+violent/ in that these features figure in the lexical items *stampede, flounder, wield, brunt* (the use of this item being another example of a category rule violation, of course) and *fling*, with which the lexical item *wind* collocates.

It is because one finds in poems features that are irregular with reference to the code but regular within the context of the poem itself that it has been proposed* that each poem might be regarded as a different language or dialect which requires a separate grammar. This proposal is intended to counter the difficulty of modifying a standard grammar to accommodate deviant sentences of the kind we have been discussing. It will be recalled that the difficulty is that if one changes the rules of a grammar so that it will generate the required sentences *The winds (were) stampeding the fields, The wind flung a magpie away*, etc., by allowing non-animate nouns to serve as subjects for the verbs *stampede, wield* and so on, then the grammar will generate a whole host of other sentences which do not have the sanction of poetic use. Examples of these might be:

> The electricity stampeded the hollyhock
> The photograph wielded the brush
> The cornfield flung a squirrel away

and so on.

Thorne's proposals are applied particularly to e e cummings' poem *anyone lived in a pretty how town* the extreme deviance of which has made it a favourite text for linguistic analysis. The poem contains lines like the following:

> anyone lived in a pretty how town
> (with up so floating many bells down)
> spring summer autumn winter
> he sang his didn't he danced his did

---

* See J. P. Thorne, 'Stylistics and Generative Grammars' in Freeman, D. C. (ed.) *Linguistics and Literary Style*, Holt, Rinehart and Winston, 1970.

Women and men (both little and small)
cared for anyone not at all
the sowed their isn't they reaped their same
sun moon stars rain

Clearly any grammar that could be fixed to generate sentences like this would generate all kinds of quite incomprehensible monstrosities. But since there is method in the apparent madness of cummings' poem it is possible to postulate certain rules which apply consistently within the text of the poem itself. Thus the indefinite noun *anyone* is, in the grammar of the poem, a Proper noun and the auxiliaries *did, didn't, isn't* become common nouns. It is because we can establish regularity in the extreme deviance of the poem that we are able to impose an interpretation upon it.

If we apply the same procedure to the poem of Ted Hughes we can set up a rule whereby the nouns *field, wind* and *stone* take on the feature / + animate/ in the 'language' represented by the poem. This would give formal linguistic recognition to the feeling one has that natural but inanimate objects, in particular the wind, are conceived of in the poem as living things. But immediately a difficulty arises. On the one hand one notices that this animacy extends to the non-natural artefact *window*, which, as we have seen is represented as trembling in the manner of a living being, but not to other artefacts like *the coal-house door*. Furthermore, there is no indication that *window* as it appears in the third line of the poem is meant to have any feature other than that it has in the language code—there is no evidence, in other words (except the doubtful evidence of identical form) that the two words are the same lexical item: they could be homonyms. Again, the feature of animacy does not extend to all other natural objects: the hills are compared expressly to a tent. And how would we specify the semantic make-up of *house*? In the fifth verse it is compared to a goblet whereas in the following verse it takes on roots like a plant.

It seems clear that it is not satisfactory to treat the text of this poem as if it were a separate language because the deviations, while regular enough to provide for interpretation, are not regular enough to be systematised as a definite code. We cannot say that nouns which are inanimate in the code become animate in the poem and we cannot even say that a particular inanimate noun operates as an animate one consistently throughout the poem. What it would seem the poet wishes to express, in fact, is the way the violent animacy of the wind infiltrates life into the very house in which he thinks to find security: the house takes on roots which move, the windows come alive. Thus the actual shift from normal code meanings to meanings which are individual to the context represents part of the message the poet is trying to convey. If we wished to set up rules for this poem as if it were a different language from standard English we would have to decide whether, for example, *window* were an animate or an inanimate noun and we cannot do this because in the poem it is, in fact, both.

The same observation applies to lexical items which are consistently different in their semantic specification from that which they have in the code. We may say the *wind* in this poem is animate, that it is represented as a living thing, but it still retains its character as an inanimate natural phenomenon. Poets cannot simply ignore the normal meanings of words and invent entirely new meanings at will since they are using a language code which already exists and upon which they depend for communication. Ted Hughes' wind in this poem is an animate one, but it must at the same time be the familiar inanimate one since this is what the lexical item *wind* means in the language. If this link with code meanings did not exist, there would of course be no way in which we could make sense of the poem.

What we see in this poem, then, is a reconciliation of contraries: the wind is required to be inanimate by reference to the code and to be animate by reference to the context. This reconciliation results in a unique lexical item which is both animate and inanimate and therefore, of course, neither one nor the other. This curious amalgam of opposites is a common feature in literary writing and, as we shall see later, is indicative of the nature of literature as discourse. Let us for the moment, however, consider other examples of it. Literary writers (as every schoolboy knows) make liberal use of the device known as personification. We can describe this in linguistic terms quite simply by saying that nouns which have the feature /−human/ in the code take on the feature /+human/ in the context of a particular literary passage. To illustrate this let us leave Ted Hughes' wind and return to that of Robert Browning in the lines quoted in the previous chapter:

> The rain set early in tonight,
> The sullen wind was soon awake,
> It tore the elm-tops down for spite,
> And did its best to vex the lake.

If we assume that sullen behaviour and spite are exclusively human attributes, then we can say that in these lines the lexical item *wind* takes on the semantic feature /+human/, that the wind is personified. But it is clear that it also remains non-human since the personal pronouns do not take on this feature: *it* (not *he* or *she*) tears the elm-tops down and does *its* (not *his* or *her*) best to vex the lake. It is almost always the case that although nouns may take on human features, the associated pronouns retain the features of the lexical item as an element of the code. The personification is seldom absolute, and it is a crucial part of the meaning of the poem in which it appears that it should not be.

Turning now to the poem of e e cummings which first inspired the proposal to treat a literary work as if it were the corpus of a different language, it becomes apparent that we cannot arrive at the meaning of the poem simply by setting up rules which make *anyone* a Proper noun, *did* a noun and so on. It is true that the context requires these recategorisations, but these words are nevertheless words of English and form part of the system of the language. Thus although *anyone* is a Proper noun it is also still an indefinite noun and the force of its use in this poem depends upon us recognising its dual character. It is a Proper noun rather as *Everyman* is a Proper noun and to ignore this fact is to miss an essential allegorical element in cummings' poem. Similarly, *did* is both a common noun and the past tense form of the 'dummy' auxiliary *do*. This auxiliary cannot of course normally occur independently but only in association with a verb: it can be said to 'carry' a feature which is common to verbs as a general category and which we might call something like /+activity/. What cummings appears to be doing when he makes *did* into a noun is to create a lexical item whose sole features are /+past/ and /+activity/. We might therefore gloss the line *he danced his did* as 'all his past activity was like a dance'. Of course this gloss does not capture the force of the original line. The paraphrase 'past activity' does not mean the same as the single invented lexical noun *did* whose sole semantic features are /+past/ and /+activity/ since this lexical item, in association with the allegorical notion of *anyone*, relates to an abstract concept of living rather than to a definite description of a particular person's life.

Let us review the points that have been made so far. An interpretation of a literary work does not depend only on the reader's knowledge of the language system or code since it is common to find uses of language which do not conform to this code and which are nevertheless interpretable. If on the other hand one sets up a grammar to describe the peculiarities of language in a particular piece of literature, thus treating it as the corpus of a different language, one does not give recognition to the fact that the ability to interpret must depend to *some* extent on the reader's knowledge of the code from which the literary language deviates. In short, neither the standard grammar nor the grammar devised for a particular literary work will account for meaning. This is because a grammar, whether it describes the language system as a whole or the language used in a particular piece of literature, can of its nature only describe *text*. What we want is a way of describing *discourse*, the manner in which linguistic elements function to communicative effect.

As has been suggested, an interpretation of a literary work as a piece of discourse involves correlating the meaning of a linguistic item as an element in the language code with the meaning it takes on in the context in which it occurs. This correlating procedure is necessary for the production and reception of any discourse, however, so that the ability to use and comprehend language as communication in general provides the basis for the understanding of literature in particular. I want now to discuss the nature of discourse comprehension in general and then show how the interpretation of literary discourse can be seen as an extension of this ability. In the second part of the book I shall then show how these notions can be applied to link the teaching of comprehension with that of literary appreciation.

It will be useful, to begin with, to make a distinction between two kinds of meaning: that which inheres in linguistic items as elements of the code on the one hand and that which linguistic items assume when they appear in contexts of use on the other. I will use the term *signification* to refer to the first kind of meaning and the term *value* to refer to the second. Let us now consider what is involved in understanding a piece of ordinary—that is to say non-literary—discourse. The following may serve as an example:

> In the north-eastern division of their territory, Bushmen bands are rather larger than elsewhere, numbering on average fifty to sixty persons and each having an hereditary headman. The members of a band are mostly relatives of the headman, together with wives who will have come originally from neighbouring bands. But the size of the group who are actually dwelling together varies from season to season and according to the accessibility of food or some exceptional circumstances. In some tribes a band breaks up in the dry season and the different households scatter in search of game, to come

together again only in the rainy season when there is an ample supply
of water and edible roots.*

We will begin with a simple observation. The entry for the word
band in a dictionary will include a wide range of meanings: a flat
strip of material, a hoop of metal or rubber, a strip forming part of
a hat or dress or shirt, a stripe of different colour or texture, a
company of armed men, robbers or musicians, a group of persons,
and so on. These meanings represent the total signification of this
word as an item in the code. The context, however, makes it clear
which of these meanings is relevant here: in other words, only one
of these meanings has the required value and the others are irrelevant.
To understand the meaning of *band* in this passage, then, the reader
has to select a meaning by matching up code and context. Notice,
however, that even if the reader did not know the signification of the
word, he would be able to derive its value from the context in which
it occurs if he knows the relevant signification of the other items.
Thus he knows from the context that a band is a number of persons,
that it has a headman, that its members are mostly relatives of the
headman, that it is a group of some kind. Most of our vocabulary is
acquired in this way by recognising what value words have: we
rarely interrupt our reading by referring to a dictionary but rely on
the context to provide us with the necessary clues. In fact when asked
the meaning of a word by some importunate child or foreigner we
tend not to adduce the signification but to give examples of value
by providing appropriate contexts.

Sometimes the recognition of value is not simply a matter of
selecting the appropriate part of the signification of a lexical item.
Consider the item *each* in the above passage, for example. A dictionary
will give something like the following signification 'every (person,
thing, group) taken separately'. This is of very little help since what
the reader wants to know is *which* person, thing or group in the
discourse the particular instance of *each* he is concerned with actually
refers to. In the present case, for example, it could refer to either
band or *person* and the reader has to decide whether it has the value
'each band' or 'each person.' Again, establishing value is frequently
a matter not of selecting a particular meaning from the semantic
complex which constitutes an item's signification but of extending it.
Here we get nearer to literary uses of language. Consider the lexical
item *break up*, for example. It may happen that the reader has only

* From Barton M., *Roles,* Tavistock Publications, 1965.

encountered this expression in reference to concrete and frangible objects (particularly if the reader is a foreign learner) so that for him this reference will constitute its signification, but if he knows the meaning of the expression in this sense he will be able to work out the 'idiomatic' value it has in this particular passage. He will do so by abstracting from the signification some feature which is appropriate to the context: in this case the feature will have to do with the disintegration of something, with the taking apart of some unity. In the code the unity is associated with a concrete mass but this association can be ignored as irrelevant in the context and the notion can be transferred to other things—in this case to a unity represented by a band of persons. The same procedure would enable him to understand the use of *break up* when this item collocates with *meeting* or *negotiation* or *family life*.

The ability of users of a language to give new values to words in actual discourse is, of course, one of the principal factors in linguistic change. Not only poets but all language users create figurative or metaphorical meanings in this way and as these meanings become accepted as part of current usage so they become part of the signification of the lexical item. To take a simple example, the terms *probe* and *freeze* are of very common occurrence in our newspapers, the first meaning *enquiry* and the second *prevention of increase (of wages)*. These meanings can be said to be part of the signification of these items now but when they were first used in these senses their value represented a figurative extension of the code meaning. As time passes and new uses enter into common custom so particular values become part of signification. This, of course, is why dictionaries have to issue appendices including not only new words but new meanings of old words which are sufficiently established for the lexicographer to accept them as part of the code of the language. It is not always easy, of course, to decide when a certain use warrants a dictionary entry: the borderline between value and signification is often hazy and what sometimes appears to be an original turn of phrase may be of general currency among a certain group of speakers.

The important point to note is the essential naturalness of metaphorical uses of language. The ability to create new values in discourse is part of what we call a person's knowledge of his language and it is not restricted to writers of literature. Grammarians sometimes talk as if it is only poets, children and foreign learners who do not conform to the rules of the language code, but as far as selection restriction rules are concerned at least very few language users are in fact strictly bound by them. It is for this reason that grammars cannot account for all aspects of language use. The widespread 'non-literal' use of language is a fact of considerable importance to the teacher of literature since it points to the possibility of representing literary works not as totally different ways of using language but as extensions of the way language is used in 'everyday' discourse. I shall develop this point later when I come to consider the teaching of literature in the second part of the book.

The question now arises: if poets (and other literary writers) only do what everybody else does, then what is distinctive about literary discourse? Essentially the distinction is that non-literal expressions occur randomly in ordinary discourse whereas in literature they figure as part of a pattern which characterises the literary work as a separate and self-contained whole. What is distinctive about a poem, for example, is that the language is organised into a pattern of recurring sounds, structures and meanings which are not determined by the phonology, syntax or semantics of the language code which provides it with its basic resources.

Consider, for example, the following verse from Tennyson's *In Memoriam:*

> He is not here; but far away
> The noise of life begins again,
> And ghastly thro' the drizzling rain
> On the bald streets breaks the blank day.

Here we have a piece of discourse which has the syntactic form of a compound sentence but which is organised phonologically in a way which is not required by the language code. It is divided into metrical lines and arranged into a rhyme scheme. The last line contains only monosyllabic words and these words are arranged so as to create a pattern of alliteration and a metrical line whose rhythm contrasts with those which precede. Over and above the code structure, then, is a linguistic organisation of the poet's own devising and this organisation is an essential part of what he is trying to convey. Except for occasional instances of onomatopoeia the actual sounds of words in a language are not significant of any particular meaning: they are meaningless elements which, when compounded, form words which *are* meaningful. Here, however, they are used to semantic effect: the monosyllabic structure of the words in the last line and the alliterative pattern they form reinforce the semantic import of the words as lexical items. The desolation that Tennyson feels is conveyed by the sound of the last line as well as by what the words themselves mean. This patterning of sound and sense into a single unit of meaning is the principal reason, of course, why translation of poetry is so extremely difficult. It is also the principal reason why para-phrase (which can be regarded as translation within one language as opposed to across two languages) must always misrepresent poetic meanings.

While it is conceivable, then, that a deviant expression like *the bald streets* or *the blank day* might occur in other forms of discourse as isolated expressions it is the manner in which they combine in this particular line and the manner in which the phonological structure of the line relates to the verse as a whole (and of course how this verse relates to the others in the poem) that characterise the use of these expressions here as literary. And they are understood not simply in terms of what value the individual words have as constituents of these phrases but of what value the phrases themselves take on as elements in a larger pattern.

It is then the correlation of code meanings, or significations, with the contextual meanings that linguistic items acquire as elements of a pattern which yields what value these items have as parts of a discourse. As we have seen in the poem of Ted Hughes previously discussed and in these lines of Tennyson a particular deviation is understood partly by reference to the code and partly by reference to the way it patterns in with the language in the rest of the poem. It should not be supposed, however, that the unique values which linguistic items take on in literary writing are dependent on deviation. Though it is common to find violations of linguistic rules in literature it is neither a necessary nor a sufficient condition for a discourse to be literary that it should be deviant as text. It is not sufficient because, as we have noted, other forms of discourse depart from code rules. it is not necessary because there is a good deal of literature which does not show any marked linguistic oddity, and which cannot be defined satisfactorily in terms of textual deviations. Consider, for example, this well-known *haiku* by Ezra Pound:

IN A STATION OF THE METRO
The apparition of these faces in the crowd;
Petals on a wet, black bough.

Here the simple juxtaposition of the two phrases leads us to associate the faces and the petals and the value of each of these lexical items in the poem derives from this association: the faces in the crowd and the petals on the wet, black bough blend to create a unique semantic image for which the language code has no term. But there is nothing in either of these noun phrases which is linguistically odd. What is odd is that in spite of the fact that they do not form a text (being two noun phrases not syntactically linked as a sentence) they do nevertheless constitute a discourse, but this is a matter I shall be taking up in the following chapter.

As another example of literary discourse which is not deviant as text we might consider the following simple poem by Robert Frost:

DUST OF SNOW

The way a crow
Shook down on me
The dust of snow
From a hemlock tree

Has given my heart
A change of mood
And saved some part
Of a day I had rued.

This poem consists of a single sentence which a grammar of English would have little problem in generating. Although there is no deviation, however, the lexical items do take on a unique value in association with each other and with their signification in the code. The word 'crow', for example, signifies a bird of the genus *Corvus*, a black bird of carrion. In this context it is associated with 'dust' and 'hemlock tree' and these words select, as it were, those features of 'crow' which they share. A hemlock tree is the common name given to *Abies Canadensis*, which is a kind of North American pine or spruce. What links the item *crow* with the item *hemlock tree* in the context of the poem, however, is not the information that the former belongs to genus *Corvus* and the latter to the genus *Abies Canadensis*, nor that the former is a bird and the latter a tree but that the crow is black and feeds on corpses and the hemlock tree is, or is thought to be because of its name, poisonous. And these features are all associated with death. The value of the item *dust* now becomes clear as the one which it has in the phrase in the burial service: 'earth to earth, ashes to ashes, dust to dust' and in the passage from *Genesis*: 'For dust thou art, and unto dust shalt thou return'.

The association of these lexical items in this context has the effect of activating those semantic features in their signification which have a common point of reference. Thus the value of each of these lexical items lies in its composite character which represents a reconciling of code and context relations. The crow is at one and the same time a familiar black-feathered bird disturbing the snow on the branches of a tree and, in relation to *dust* and *hemlock* in the poem, a symbol of death. Once this basic value is recognised, one can then go on to impose a more specific interpretation on the poem and suggest that the crow represents a black-frocked priest scattering dust on a coffin. Since poetic meanings are of their very nature unspecific and ambiguous it is always possible for the reader to translate them into precise terms and so adapt them to his own personal vision: there is no such thing as a definitive interpretation. What is important, however (particularly from the teaching point of view) is that the individual interpretation should be based on an understanding of how linguistic items take on particular values in discourse. I shall return to this point, and to this poem, in Chapter 6.

Literary discourse then is characterised by the creation of language patterns over and above those which are required by the linguistic code and these patterns bestow upon the linguistic items within them certain meanings which, when fused with the signification these items have as code elements, constitute their unique semantic value. I have tried to show how these patterns are formed by phonological means and by the semantic links between individual lexical items. I want now to discuss the patterning of syntactic structures. We can begin with a simple example from Alexander Pope:

> See how the world its veterans rewards!
> A youth of frolics, an old age of cards;
> Fair to no purpose, artful to no end,
> Young without lovers, old without a friend . . .

Each of the last three lines here consists of two structurally equivalent phrases. Furthermore, the syntactic equivalence is reinforced by semantic links between the lexical items which appear in these structures. Thus *youth* and *old age* are semantically linked as antonyms by virtue of their signification, as of course are *young* and *old*. *Frolics* and *cards* are synonymously related under a general semantic feature such as /+entertainment/ and *lovers* and *friend* are similarly related under some feature such as /+affection/. *Purpose* and *end* are synonyms. It should be noted that in this pattern of syntactic and semantic equivalence, synonymous expressions appear in each case as the second part of each phrase and that these are balanced in the second and fourth lines by antonymous expressions

D

relating to the dichotomy of youth and age. Two items, however, do not fit into this scheme by virtue of their signification: these are the terms *fair* and *artful* occurring in the third line. Now there is no explicit indication whether this line is meant to refer to the 'veterans' in their youth or in their age. But the position in the pattern of these two terms suggests that they are related in the same way as *youth/old age* and *young/old* are related. That is to say, the expressions *fair* and *artful* are conditioned by the context so that they take on particular values: fairness is represented as a quality associated with youth and artfulness as a quality associated with age. We might go on to suggest that the picture that emerges is of women practising the art of coquetry after they have lost the youth and beauty which would enable them to succeed.

What I am suggesting is that a pattern of structural equivalences can condition the lexical items in the structures concerned in such a way that they take on meanings other than those they have in the language code. Here is another example of this happening:

AN IRISH AIRMAN FORESEES HIS DEATH

I know that I shall meet my fate
Somewhere among the clouds above;
Those that I fight I do not hate,
Those that I guard I do not love;
My country is Kiltartan Cross,
My countrymen Kiltartan's poor,
No likely end could bring them loss
Or leave them happier than before.
Nor law, nor duty bade me fight,
Nor public men, nor cheering crowds,
A lonely impulse of delight
Drove to this tumult in the clouds;
I balanced all, brought all to mind,
The years to come seemed waste of breath,
A waste of breath the years behind
In balance with this life, this death.

                                                    (Yeats)

The third and fourth lines of this poem are exactly equivalent from the structural point of view: they also have the same rhythm. This structural and phonological identity has the effect of implying a sameness of meaning. But the two verbs in each of the lines are direct antonyms: *fight/guard* and *hate/love*. In respect to the code, therefore, the two lexical items are opposite in meaning but the context neutralises the opposition and the two items are conditioned into equivalence. With reference to signification, then, we can say that the two sentences express complementary propositions, but with reference to the value suggested by the equivalence of form and rhythm, the propositions are the same. For the Irish airman, we might suggest, fighting those you do not hate amounts to the same thing as guarding those you do not love, and, further, that fighting amounts to the same thing as guarding and hating is not distinct from loving: love, hate, law, duty and patriotism are reduced to the same meaning and so are equally meaningless. The fatalism which leads him to equate love and hate leads him ultimately in the last line to equate the ultimate opposites life and death.

As a further example of the way structural equivalence can condition meaning let us consider the following extract from E. M. Forster's novel *A Passage to India**:

> The Ganges, though flowing from the foot of Vishnu and through Siva's hair, is not an ancient stream. Geology, looking further than religion, knows of a time when neither the river nor the Himalayas that nourished it existed, and an ocean flowed over the holy places of Hindustan. The mountains rose, their debris silted up the ocean, the gods took their seats on them and contrived the river, and the India we call immemorial came into being. But India is really far older. In the days of the prehistoric ocean the southern part of the peninsula already existed, and the high places of Dravidia have been land since land began, and have seen on the one side the sinking of a continent that joined them to Africa, and on the other the upheaval of the Himalayas from a sea.

This description of India is part mystical and part geological and the two are inextricably blended: the formation of the mountains and the consequent silting up of the ocean are described in the same compound sentence as the gods taking their seats and bringing the river into being. *The mountains rose* is at one level of structure equivalent to *the gods took their seats* and *their debris silted up the ocean* equivalent to (*they*) *contrived the river* and these structural equivalences, included as they are within one sentence, suggest that these activities are of the same kind. What seems to be implied is that in India natural and supernatural events are indistinguishable and this of course is an underlying theme of the book as a whole. Another instance of structural equivalence reinforces this theme. The two phrases *the holy places of Hindustan* and *the high places of Dravidia* are syntactically identical and have the same lexical item as the head of the nominal group (*places*). This similarity has the

* E. M. Forster, *A Passage to India*, E. J. Arnold, 1924.

effect of equating the high places, which refer to geology, and the holy places, which refer to religion. They are represented as aspects of the same complex concept of India and may be said to express on a small scale the same theme as is reflected in the general structure of the novel itself: Part I: Mosque, Part II: Caves, Part III: Temple. 'Only connect!'

At the heart of literary creation is the struggle to devise patterns of language which will bestow upon the linguistic items concerned just those values which convey the individual writer's personal vision. In the cases we have been considering, the struggle is not evident but in other cases the actual process of creating value is represented in the discourse itself. The struggle is both described and exemplified in the following lines from T. S. Eliot's *Four Quartets*:*

> Words strain,
> Crack and sometimes break, under the burden,
> Under the tension, slip, slide, perish,
> Decay with imprecision, will not stay in place,
> Will not stay still.   (Burnt Norton)

Here we have a sentence consisting of a subject noun phrase (*Words*) and a whole series of verb phrases which, by virtue of the fact that they share the same subject, are at one level of structure equivalent. What these verb phrases represent is a number of features of some non-existent verb, aspects of a concept for which the code provides no lexical item. The value of each of these verbal groups then is that it realises an element in a semantic compound which the poet conceptualises but cannot explicitly state. What these lines both describe and express is the poet 'trying to learn to use words', trying to manipulate the language code to convey notions for which the code has no terms. This, of course, is a recurrent theme in *Four Quartets*:†

> . . . one has only learnt to get the better of words
> For the thing one no longer has to say, or the way in which
> One is no longer disposed to say it.   (East Coker)

But it is also the essential predicament of the literary writer in general: the code does not provide for the expression of his individual perceptions and concepts so he has to devise his own patterns of language to give words the value of individual meanings.

This search for expressions which will have just the value required

---

* T. S. Eliot, *Four Quartets* (Burnt Norton), Faber and Faber, 1959.
† T. S. Eliot, *Four Quartets* (East Coker), Faber and Faber, 1959

to convey the writer's meaning is particularly evident in the writing
of Wordsworth and D. H. Lawrence. In both we find meanings
conveyed by a kind of cumulative effect as the writer expresses, in
a series of equivalent structures, the semantic features which together
constitute the total impression of the concept he wishes to convey.
We actually witness what Eliot calls 'the intolerable wrestle/With
words and meanings'. Consider these well-known lines from
Wordsworth's *Tintern Abbey*:

> And I have felt
> A presence that disturbs me with the joy
> Of elevated thoughts; a sense sublime
> Of Something far more deeply interfused,
> 5 Whose dwelling is the light of setting suns,
> And the round ocean and the living air,
> And the blue sky, and in the mind of man;
> A motion and a spirit, that impels
> All thinking things, all objects of all thought,
> 10 And rolls through all things.

These lines consist of one sentence: subject (*I*) verb (*have felt*)
and an object consisting of three noun phrases in parallel, each
being therefore structurally equivalent to the others at the most
immediate level of analysis. Each of these phrases represents an
attempt to capture an elusive sensation which is both a presence
and a sense, both a motion and a spirit, an experience which is
compounded of all these and at the same time manifested through
each of them. We do not get a precise image of what it is that the
poet has felt since the language code provides no means of making
it precise: we get a number of its features which suggest its character.
It is part presence, part spirit, part sense and part motion: all of
these and yet none of them.

We have a similar repetition of equivalent structures within the
second of these noun phrases. Thus *the light of setting suns, the round
ocean, the living air* and so on are all noun phrases operating as
complements in the embedded sentence 'The dwelling is . . .'. Again
the sameness of syntactic position suggests an equivalence of value:
this 'something' resides in the setting sun, the ocean, the air, the
sky and the mind of man and each of these is equivalent as a dwelling-
place for this 'something' but at the same time this dwelling-place
is only *manifested* here: its essential character is beyond exact
description. This 'something' must be inferred: it is itself of its very
nature ineffable.

Wordsworth's struggle to express the inexpressible is, then, directly reflected in the structure of his verse. The patterns of equivalences within equivalences represent the very search for the expression which will capture the experience. It has often been observed that Wordsworth achieves a 'poetic' effect with the absolute minimum of 'poetic' devices: often the words he uses are almost semantically empty—*something, objects, things* and his collocations are common to the point of banality: *the light of setting suns, the round ocean, the blue sky.* The effect of his poetry can often, I think, be traced to the manner in which the very patterning of equivalent structures in his verse suggests the urgent search for a way of expressing what is beyond the limits of normal language use. In the lines from *Tintern Abbey* that we have been considering we have a simple proposition: 'I have felt X' and the nine lines which follow explore ways in which this X might be expressed.

Notice, too, how the reader is involved in the exploration. He brings to his reading of the poem a knowledge of the language code and this inevitably provides him with a set of predictions about how the linguistic structure will develop. When he comes to the end of the first line, for example, he will predict the occurrence of an object for the verb *felt* since his knowledge of grammar tells him that this is a transitive verb and that without an object noun phrase the sentence is incomplete. The noun phrase *A presence that disturbs me with the joy of elevated thoughts* completes the sentence and fulfils the reader's syntactic prediction. But now the context itself develops a linguistic pattern of repetition as another object noun phrase appears and this reaches syntactic completion at the end of line 4. At this point the reader anticipates a continuation of the pattern established by the repeated noun phrases but his prediction is proved wrong since what we get is an elaboration of the second noun phrase by means of a relative clause. Another pattern then emerges with the repeated object noun phrases of this embedded sentence: *the light of setting suns, and the round ocean,* and so on. The reader adjusts his prediction to the new pattern. At the end of line 7 this pattern comes to an end and the reader might imagine that the structure is complete: all code and context predictions have been satisfied. But the next line returns him to the main sentence again as a third object noun phrase appears long after the prediction of its occurrence has been deflected by the pattern of repeated noun phrases in the relative clause embedded in the second main object noun phrase.

The effect of all this is to create expectations in the reader and then deny him their satisfaction; to remove him, as it were, from the predictable world into uncertainty and thus to involve him in the exploration of the elusive mystical experience which the poet is attempting to express. The elusiveness of the syntactic patterning in these lines becomes part of the elusiveness of the message that the lines convey. In this sense, the meaning of this passage from *Tintern Abbey* lies in the very manner in which the syntax is organised. But notice that although the syntax is elaborate the lexis is simple: as has already been pointed out the collocations are banal in their predictability. We thus get a contrast between on the one hand the elaborate patterning of the syntax which defeats prediction and leaves the reader in suspense, as it were, from the certainties of the everyday world and on the other hand the very simple lexis which expresses what is familiar and ordinary in the reader's experience. It is through this contrast, which characterises so much of Wordsworth's style, that his essential vision is expressed: the simplest and most common-place objects of nature take on the value of mysterious revelations and 'the meanest flower that blows' and the 'wisdom and spirit of the universe' become one.

As has already been suggested, we find in the writings of D. H. Lawrence a similar use of patterns of syntactic equivalence which express the process of trying to capture a fugitive meaning. Here, for example, is an extract from *The Rainbow*:

> She wanted to get out of this fixed, leaping, forward-travelling move-ment, to rise from it as a bird rises with wet, limp feet from the sea, to lift herself as a bird lifts its breast and thrusts its body from the pulses and heave of the sea that bears it forward to an unwilling conclusion, tear herself away like a bird on wings, and in the open space where there is clarity, rise up above the fixed, surcharged motion, separate speck that hangs suspended, moves this way and that, seeing and answering before it sinks again, having chosen or found the direction in which it shall be carried forward.

Here we have one immensely elaborated sentence in which there are a series of verb phrases (each therefore equivalent at the most immediate level) which are themselves elaborated into patterns of equivalence. The structure of the passage is basically:

	.	get out of—movement
	.	rise—sea
She wanted to	.	lift herself—conclusion
	.	tear herself away—clarity
	.	rise up—forward

These verbs are all very similar in meaning and can be said to have the same basic signification in the code but each time one is used its value in the context is extended so that the rising up is like the action of a bird rising from the sea, and then like a bird not simply rising but making an effort to lift itself, to tear itself away from the constraining sea, and then like a bird freely suspended in the air. Structures, equivalent on one level, become increasingly elaborate in the attempt to provide an expression which will suggest just what it is that Anna Brangwen feels. And this struggle with the language directly represents her struggle for emotional freedom. We do not get any precise image of Anna's feelings since the code provides no way of specifying what they are. Instead the repetitions and the elaborations which create patterns which defy prediction (in the same way as do Wordsworth's lines) express the feelings directly in all their immediacy: as Wordsworth puts it in *The Prelude*:

> the soul
> Remembering how it felt but what it felt
> Remembering not.

What I have tried to show in this chapter is that meaning in literary works is not simply a function of the signification that linguistic items have as code elements but a function of the relationship between this signification and the value these items take on as elements in a pattern created in the context. That is to say, we interpret literature not as text but as discourse. But all discourse is interpreted by correlating code and context: what distinguishes our understanding of literary discourse is that it depends on our recognising patterns of linguistic organisation which are superimposed as it were on those which the code requires, and on our inferring the special values that linguistic items contract as elements in these created patterns.

I have discussed how the patterning of language in a literary work sets up a system of regularities and how a recognition of these regularities contributes to interpretation. A question which has been touched upon from time to time but not explored is: why does the literary writer go to this trouble? What does the poet or the writer of fiction hope to achieve by working the language into these unique and distinctive designs? What kind of communication does literary discourse represent? These questions are taken up in the following chapter.

4

The nature
of literary communication

It was observed in the preceding chapter that although it is quite
common to find deviant sentences in literary writing, deviance of this
linguistic kind is not a defining feature of literature. What does
seem crucial to the character of literature is that the language of a
literary work should be fashioned into patterns over and above those
required by the actual language system. Whether the components
of these patterns are deviant or non-deviant or both is of secondary
importance. What I want to suggest now is that the effect of this
patterning is to create acts of communication which are self-contained
units, independent of a social context and expressive of a reality
other than that which is sanctioned by convention. In other words,
I want to suggest that although literature need not be deviant as
text it must of its nature be deviant as discourse.

We will begin by considering what constitutes a normal communication situation. Typically we have a sender transmitting a signal to a
receiver. Sending, transmitting and receiving are terms which refer
to the process of communication as a physical operation. In social
terms we have an addresser who directs a message to an addressee.
In normal circumstances the sender and addresser are one, as are the
receiver and addressee. The person who transmits an acoustic signal
is doing the addressing and the person whose ears pick up the signal
is the person being addressed. Similarly, the person who initiates the
transmitting of a written message form (whether this passes via the
secretary's short-hand notebook or not) is the addresser and the
person who reads it is the one to whom the message is addressed.
One can think of exceptions to this general rule like eavesdropping,
telephone tapping, opening other people's mail and so on but notice
that these are usually regarded as aberrant and anti-social activities.
Standard social practice (in most societies at least) is for the sender/
addresser and the receiver/addressee to be identical.

Grammatically the sender/addresser is the first person and the receiver/addressee the second person. These are participant roles in the communication situation. In addition we have the third person which denotes someone/something referred to but not engaged in the interaction.

Let us now consider a few instances of literary discourse:

> I am the enemy you killed, my friend . . .   (Owen)

> I am not yet born; O hear me.
> Let not the bloodsucking bat or the rat or the stoat or
> the club-footed ghoul come near me.   (MacNeice)

> I come from haunts of coot and hern . . .   (Tennyson)

> I bring fresh showers for the thirsting flowers,
>   From the seas and the streams;
> I bear light shade for the leaves when laid
>   in their noonday dreams.   (Shelley)

What is immediately apparent in the first two of these extracts is that the first person pronoun cannot be referring to the actual initiator of the message since the basic requirement we make of a sender is that he should be alive. Corpses and foetuses are not eligible. Another requirement is that the sender should be human. In the third extract, however, the first person pronoun refers not to Tennyson but to a brook and in the fourth it refers not to Shelley but to a cloud. The senders of these messages, then, are the poets Owen, MacNeice, Tennyson and Shelley: they have actually put pen to paper to produce these lines. The addressers, however, are a corpse, a foetus, a brook and a cloud, all of which are naturally *third* person objects: things which are referred to and not people who actually participate in the communication situation. The normal amalgam of sender/addresser is therefore dissolved: it is not the sender who is doing the addressing and not the addresser who is doing the sending. The first person pronoun in these extracts, then, is not the conventional one but is somehow compounded with the third person to create a unique kind of reference. The dissolving of the amalgam which provides the reference for the conventional first person results in the creation of an amalgam of first and third person reference. The 'I' of these extracts is both first person (as the addresser) and third person (as a non-human or inanimate object incapable of participating in communication).

Let us now consider how the second person works in literary discourse:

Ye trees! whose slender roots entwine
   Altars that piety neglects . . .   (Wordsworth)

Thou still unravish'd bride of quietness,
   Thou foster-child of silence and slow time . . .   (Keats)

With how sad steps, O moon, thou climbst the skies . . .
                                           (Sidney)

In the three extracts here the addressees are inanimate objects
incapable of receiving messages and naturally, therefore, third person
entities. We do not normally talk to trees, Grecian urns and the
heavenly bodies with any expectation that they actually understand
and are likely to respond to what we are saying. Poets very commonly
address non-human objects—birds, flowers, mountains, the seasons
of the year and so on—but they know that it is the human reader
who actually receives their messages. It would seem, then, that the
second person in literary writing is again different from the conventional second person in that it refers to an addressee who is not
the receiver. Again the normally indivisible compound of receiver/
addressee is dissolved and as a result the second person pronoun
takes on an additional third person meaning.

    What I am suggesting is that the first and second person pronouns in
literary writing take on a unique value which is a blend of the normal
signification of first and third persons and second and third persons
respectively. If we wanted to convert the extracts that have been
cited to normal discourse we would have to change the pronouns into
the third person to yield, for example:

    He is not yet born. . . .
    It comes from haunts of coot and hern. . . .
    The still unravish'd bride of quietness. . . .

and so on. But then the value of the discourse is altered: the poet is
no longer 'saying the same thing'. We might express the difference
for the moment by saying that the immediacy of the experience is
lost and the poet is detached from complete involvement. Later I
shall try to give a more precise account of how the discourse differs.

    We have seen how the third person is drawn into participation
by combining with the first and second persons in literary discourse
thus giving the pronouns conventionally associated with these persons
a unique value. The question now arises: how does the third person
pronoun itself operate in literature? Let us consider an example:

Fear took hold of him. Gripping tightly to the lamp, he reeled, and
looked round. The water was carrying his feet away, he was dizzy.

He did not know which way to turn. The water was whirling, whirling, the whole black night was swooping in rings. He swayed uncertainly at the centre of all the attack, reeling in dismay. In his soul, he knew he would fall.

As he staggered something in the water struck his legs, and he fell. Instantly he was in the turmoil of suffocation, fighting, wrestling, but always borne down, borne inevitably down. Still he wrestled and fought to get himself free, in the unutterable struggle of suffocation, but he always fell again deeper. Something struck his head, a great wonder of anguish went over him, then the blackness covered him entirely.

In the utter darkness, the unconscious, drowning body was rolled along, the water pouring, washing, filling in the place. The cattle woke up and rose to their feet, the dog began to yelp.

(D. H. Lawrence: *The Rainbow*)

What has to be noticed here is that Lawrence is describing the sensations of a drowning man which are of their very nature not accessible to observation and which cannot therefore in normal circumstances be predicated of a third person, unless reported speech is used. Such a direct description of what goes on in the mind and the nervous system can only be appropriately given in the first person: 'Fear took hold of *me* . . .', 'In *my* soul, *I* knew *I* would fall . . .' and so on. But of course it will not do to alter the pronouns in this passage to make them conform to conventional usage because the person described here (Tom Brangwen) drowns and he is not represented as a ghost speaking from beyond the grave. So neither the first nor, the third person is appropriate in its conventional sense. What in effect we have in this passage is the third person pronoun which takes on the value of both the third and the first persons. Sometimes it is the former which appears to predominate as when we have a description of events which are open to observation in the normal way: *Gripping tightly to the lamp, he reeled, and looked round . . . The cattle woke up and rose to their feet, the dog began to yelp . . .* and so on. At other times it is the first person which is, as it were, in focus, as when we have an account of Tom Brangwen's actual feelings. But it does not strike us that there is any incongruity in this since we recognise that the pronoun is not used in its code sense but assumes a unique value in this context.

It would appear then that in literary discourse we do not have a sender addressing a message directly to a receiver, as is normally the case. Instead we have a communication situation within a communication situation and a message whose meaning is self-contained and not dependent on who sends it and who receives it. The value of 'I' and 'you' (or 'thou' or 'ye') derives partly from

what these pronouns refer to in the code, that is to say addresser and
addressee respectively, and partly from the acquisition of third
person features which are bestowed upon them by the context. The
consequence of this is that a piece of literary discourse is in suspense
from the usual process of social interaction whereby senders address
messages directly to receivers. The literary message does not arise
in the normal course of social activity as do other messages, it arises
from no previous situation and requires no response, it does not serve
as a link between people or as a means of furthering the business of
ordinary social life. We might represent the normal communication
situation as follows:

III

I
Sender
Addresser

II
Receiver
Addressee

The situation which obtains in literary discourse, on the other hand,
appears to be as follows:

I/III II/III
Sender Addresser Addressee Receiver

There are three objections which might be raised against this
characterisation of literary communication. The first is that pronouns in English commonly refer to more than one person anyway
so there is nothing unusual about the way they are used in literary
discourse. Now, it is true that the *plural* first person may have the signification I + III as when it includes the speaker and one or more
people who are not being directly addressed. An example would be:

My wife has a train to catch so we must leave at once.

'We' may also include speaker and hearer (I + II) as when the
husband addresses his wife and says:

Your train leaves at 10 so we must leave at once.

Again, 'we' may include all three persons (I + II + III) as when the
husband says:

Your train leaves at 10. Call the children, we must leave at once.

Similarly, the plural 'you' may be II + II when there is more than
one addressee or II + III when people not directly addressed are
also included. But the plural pronouns have what we can call
multiple reference, which we might represent by the formulae I + II,

I + III and so on. What I have been discussing are singular pronouns which in the code can only have *single* reference but which in literary writing have what we might call *compound* reference. This we might represent by the formulae I/III, II/III, III/I, where the first number indicates the feature of the actual pronoun form and the second the additional feature with which it is compounded. Singular compound pronouns do not refer to one person plus another person but one person which is a unique blend of what is normally distinguished as two persons, which is neither of them and both of them at the same time. It is the use of pronouns of this value which is unique to literary discourse.

The second objection is that although one can cite instances of pronouns which in a way may be said to be compounded of different persons (as I have done) it does not follow that all literature makes use of pronouns in this way. There are many cases, particularly in lyric poetry (the objector might continue) where the first person pronoun clearly does refer to the poet who is both sender and addresser. This objection is rather more difficult to counter. I would do so, however, by suggesting that the examples I have cited (and one could cite innumerable others) are representative of literary discourse in the sense that even if the first and second person pronouns do not refer to entities which cannot of their nature send and receive messages, they do nevertheless depend for their value on the dissolution of the sender/addresser and receiver/addressee amalgams and on the addition of a third person feature. To see why this should be so one has to consider what role is assumed by the literary writer. In all forms of written discourse, with the exception of the diary and the personal letter (which I will come to presently) the sender/addresser adopts a recognised role: lawyer, civil servant, businessman, journalist, teacher and so on. What he says, and how he says it, is to a large extent determined by the role that he adopts and he is not at liberty to express his own individual sentiments at will. Nor indeed does he have the occasion to do so since his addressee will be concerned with what he has to say in his role and not with his private and individual thoughts. Such thoughts are part of the idiosyncratic and secret lives of people as individuals which find no expression in the public roles they assume as social beings. We may say that the 'I' of conventional communication refers to the social persona and not to the individual person.

The 'I' in literary writing, on the other hand, does refer to the private thoughts, impressions, imaginings and perceptions of the individual person. They are brought out of hiding, as it were, and objectified and it is the literary writer who does the objectifying by fashioning the appropriate message form. But it is not the writer as the message sender, the craftsman, the 'maker' that the 'I' refers to but to the inner self that the writer is objectifying, and the very act of objectification involves detaching this self and observing it as if it were a third person entity. It may, indeed, not correspond to the real self of the writer at all but to experiences which he imagines himself undergoing. We cannot assume that when a literary writer uses the first person pronoun he is describing his own actual experiences or making a confession. We cannot assume, in other words, that the sender and the addresser are one.

The literary writer is, of course, well aware that the artistic convention within which he works allows for this distinction between sender and addresser and so relieves him from any social responsibility for what he says in the first person. This is how literary writing differs from diaries and personal letters. In the latter there is no distinction between sender and addresser and the writer is assumed to be 'telling the truth', describing real events, expressing his own feelings. Thus diaries and personal letters can be incriminating and can be used as evidence in a court of law: love letters can involve the sender in an action for breach of promise, but love poems do not count as binding in the same way. I would wish to claim, then, that the literary writer always works within the framework of the detached communication situation that has been described, even when the framework itself is not immediately evident. As a writer he has no direct social role to play.

The point about the literary writer's lack of social role brings us to the third objection. It may be objected that the writer frequently does have a social purpose: to reform society, to make a plea for tolerance, to inspire political action and so on. The answer to this objection is that it may indeed be the purpose of a writer to stir the social conscience but he does not do so by addressing himself directly to those whose consciences he wishes to stir. He expresses a certain reality, a personal vision, and the reader, as an *observer* of this reality, might then feel constrained to act in a certain way. But he is not directed to act by the writer. Hasek's novel *The Good Soldier Schweik* may have inspired a nation to rebel against oppression, and Styron's novel *The Confessions of Nat Turner* may provoke a sense of gross social injustice but these are novels and not political pamphlets and whatever social effect they have, powerful though it may be, must be indirect. And of course as novels their effect cannot be measured in terms of the action they provoke: a political pamphlet or a religious tract fails if it does not inspire the reader to behave in a certain way, but the success of a literary work does not at all depend on a resulting activity. Most literature provokes no social action whatever. Shelley spoke of poets as 'the unacknowledged legislators of the world', but a legislator who is not acknowledged is not a legislator: poets do not make laws, although they may indirectly influence those that do.

I would claim, then, that it is of the nature of literary communication to be dissociated from the immediate social context. Literary discourse is independent of normal interaction, has no links with any preceding discourse and anticipates no subsequent activity either verbal or otherwise. Its interpretation does not depend on its being placed in a context of situation or on our recognition of the role of the sender or our own role as receiver. It is a self-contained whole, interpretable internally, as it were, as a self-contained unit of communication, and in suspense from the immediate reality of social life.

It is because a literary work is dissociated from other social interaction that the writer is required to work the language into patterns. Since a literary work does not link up with other discourse it has to be designed so as to be self-contained and the very design, the creation of unique patterns of language, inevitably reflects a reality other than that which is communicable by conventional uses of the language code. Consider, for example, the following short poem by Roethke:

CHILD ON TOP OF A GREENHOUSE

The wind billowing out the seat of my britches,
My feet crackling splinters of glass and dried putty,
The half-grown chrysanthemums staring up like accusers,
Up through the streaked glass, flashing with sunlight,
A few white clouds all rushing eastward,
A line of elms plunging and tossing like horses,
And everyone, everyone pointing up and shouting.

If we consider this poem as text we can describe it by saying that it consists of a series of noun phrases, or nominal groups, and we can account for its deviance in grammatical terms by saying that it is a 'sentence' which lacks the obligatory category of verb phrase (VP). That is to say, the poem begins with a capital and ends with a full stop and is represented as an independent utterance, but independent utterances must be related to sentences and here there is no sentence but only a collection of noun phrases. The first base rule of a generative grammar is:

S→NP+VP

In the poem, however, the required rule would appear to be:

S→NP+NP etc.

It is, of course, common to find utterances which consist only of noun phrases but the important point to note is that such utterances are not independent but relatable to a foregoing utterance which provides the grammatical elements necessary for a sentence to be reconstituted. For example, the first line of the poem could serve as a reply to a question as in the following exchange:

A: What do you feel?
B: The wind billowing out the seat of my britches.

Here B's remark is an utterance consisting of a noun phrase, but A's question provides the means whereby the utterance can be related to the sentence:

I feel the wind billowing out the seat of my britches.

Thus we can say that underlying B's utterance is a sentence consisting of a noun phrase (*I*) and a verb phrase (*feel the wind etc.*) and further that the verb phrase consists of a verb (*feel*) and another noun phrase (*the wind etc.*). We can show this in a simple diagram as follows:

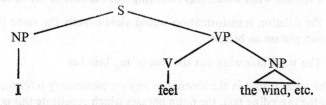

In the poem, however, there is no way of relating the noun phrases to a sentence of which they are constituents because we have no previous linguistic material from which to derive the necessary grammatical information.

Notice that one piece of grammatical information that the foregoing text provides is tense. In the exchange between A and B that was cited, the tense of the verb in A's question is transferred to the main sentence which underlies B's reply, and also to the sentence

E

which is embedded in the object noun phrase of that sentence. As we saw in Chapter 2, the modifying and qualifying elements in a noun phrase can be shown as deriving from embedded sentences which at the first stage of transformational treatment may become relative clauses but which can also be further treated to result in preposed adjectives or qualifying phrases. In the case of B's reply, for example, we can say that the deep structure of the sentence which underlies it takes something like the following form:

I feel the wind/the wind is billowing out the seat of my britches.

Transformational treatment will then yield alternative surface forms like:

I feel the wind which is billowing out the seat of my britches.
I feel the wind billowing out the seat of my britches.

But notice that B's remark could take exactly the same form even if A's question made use of a past tense of the verb. If A's question were:

A: What *did* you feel?

then B's utterance would be related to an underlying sentence of the form:

I *felt* the wind/the wind *was* billowing out the seat of my britches.

The relative clause transformation would then yield:

I felt the wind which was billowing out the seat of my britches.

and the deletion transformation would yield exactly the same form of noun phrase as before:

The wind billowing out the seat of my britches.

The point is that in the absence of any supplementary information from the preceding text, the noun phrases which constitute this poem have no specific time reference. We do not know whether we are to understand 'The wind (is) billowing out the seat of my britches etc.' or 'The wind (was) billowing out the seat of my britches, etc.' or even 'The wind (will be) billowing out the seat of my britches etc.' What in effect we have is aspect without tense and this is something which is not normally possible. In the system of the language aspect and tense are interrelated and one cannot have one without the other: indeed, we talk of present continuous and present perfect *tenses* thereby including aspect as a feature of the general category tense. But in this poem what is normally inseparable becomes separated: we have aspect but no tense.

So far we have been pointing out certain linguistic peculiarities of this poem as a text. What relevance do they have for an understanding of the poem as a discourse, as an act of communication? The effect of isolating aspect here is to make a statement about a sensation of ongoing movement which has no attachment to time. The boy is perched on top of a greenhouse, physically aloof from the world below and at the same time removed from the reality which it represents, detached from real time and aware only of a kind of timeless movement. And this sensation of duration outside time is expressed by the recurrence of the progressive form which runs as a motif through the linguistic patterning of the poem—*billowing, crackling, staring, flashing, rushing, plunging, tossing, pointing, shouting.*

The reality which the poem records is that of subjective impression. It is a reality which cannot be expressed by normal language usage since this can of its nature only express that reality which is accepted by shared social convention. Individual thoughts, feelings and perceptions, the private person that lies beneath the public persona, can only be fully expressed by going beyond the limits of what is conventionally communicable. But this reality is not of course unrelated to that which is sanctioned by society as a whole, so the expression of this reality draws on the resources of the language code and uses them to create patterns of its own.

Although, as we have seen, there are many different ways in which the resources of the code are used to create the idiosyncratic and self contained patterns of language which characterise literary discourse, one can distinguish a general strategy which underlies them. This can be put simply as follows: combine what is kept separate in the code and separate what is combined in the code. An instance of the former is the manner in which semantic features which are opposites combine to form hybrid units of meaning which reconcile the contraries. As was demonstrated in the preceding chapter, for example, a lexical item can combine the feature /−human/ which is part of its signification with the feature /+human/ which the context imposes upon it, thus creating a unique value whereby the entity referred to is both human and not human at the same time. In the code the features /−human/ and /+human/ are kept clearly distinct, but in literary writing it is common to find them conflated, thus creating referents which have no place in conventional reality. Something is either human or not human, it cannot be both: but in literature it can.

Another instance of the way literary writing combines what is conventionally distinct is the fusing of what linguists refer to as double articulation or double structure. What this means, in essence, is that the units which comprise the phonological structure of language have no independent function but serve only to construct units of grammar. Put simply, sounds themselves only become significant when they combine to form words. But we have seen that in poetry the patterns of sound which the writer devises do have a function other than that of constructing words: they enter directly into the meaning by providing lexical items with a value which they would not otherwise have. The following may have very much the same signification as sentences:

> The murmurous haunt of flies on summer eves.   (Keats)
> The presence of the murmuring noise of flies on evenings of summer.

but the second does not have the same value as the first: there is not the same degree of 'convergence' of double structure.

This combination of the two distinct levels of linguistic structure represents a quite fundamental reformulation of the principles upon which language is organised. But literary discourse not only effaces the distinction between the two levels of description but also the distinction between the two kinds of relation which the units at these levels enter into. A linguistic unit, whether a 'sound' at the phonological level or a 'word' or 'group of words' at the grammatical level, enters into two kinds of relation: it is *paradigmatically* related to units which can occur in the same phonological or grammatical context, and *syntagmatically* related to units which it actually does occur with and which constitute this phonological or grammatical context. To take a simple example from the phonological level, the sound /p/ (we can call it a sound for the purposes of this discussion though for a linguist this term lacks precision) occurs in words like *pet*, *pat* and *pack* so that the sounds represented by *-et*, *-at* and *-ack* co-occur with it and constitute its possible phonological contexts: that is to say, it is in syntagmatic relationship with these sounds. The sound /b/ can also occur in these contexts to produce the words *bet*, *bat* and *back*. /p/ and /b/, therefore, have the same potentiality of occurrence in the contexts *-et*, *-at*, and *-ack* and in consequence are in paradigmatic relationship with each other.

To make certain that the distinction is clear, let us see how it operates at the grammatical level. Take the following sentence:

The plumber smiled.

Here we have a sentence consisting of an NP (*The plumber*) and a VP (*smiled*). Now innumerable other items can occur as the NP: 'The baker/ My aunt Charlotte/ An old man who happened to be passing/ smiled.' Since all of these can occur at this place in structure they are all in paradigmatic relationship. Similarly, there are innumerable items which can occur as a VP instead of 'smiled', including, for example, 'complained', 'arrived', 'mended the pipes', 'installed a new bath'. All of these are verb phrases or VPs but we can establish paradigms at a more refined level of linguistic structure: we can set up a class of intransitive verbs which are all verbs having no following NP as part of their grammatical environment. Then we can say that 'complained' and 'arrived' are paradigmatically related but 'arrived' and 'installed' or 'complained' and 'mended' are not. The verbs 'mend' and 'install' cannot occur in a grammatical context which provides no following NP: 'The plumber installed' and 'The plumber mended' are ungrammatical sentences. Similarly the verbs 'complain' and 'arrive' cannot occur in the context required for transitive verbs. We cannot have 'The plumber arrived the pipes' or 'The plumber complained a new bath'.

To put the matter simply, a sound or a word or a phrase is in paradigmatic relation with any other which can replace it and the context which provides the position in which these different elements can operate consists of items which are in syntagmatic relation with these elements and with each other. To make (or 'generate') a correct grammatical sentence one selects an element from one paradigmatic set, and combines it with one from another: one selects an NP— 'The plumber', 'The boy next door', 'The Queen'—and then combines it with a selected VP—'installed the lavatory', 'sat on a thistle', 'had lunch with the Pope'. And of course within the NP and the VP there are other paradigmatic choices: between Proper and common nouns, and within the class of common nouns between count and non-count nouns, animate and non-animate nouns; and within the VP transitive and intransitive verbs belong to different paradigms.

These facts are well known to foreign language teachers (though not perhaps in this particular terminological guise) and provide the basis for the well-known substitution table where the items on the horizontal plane are syntagmatically related and those on the vertical plane are paradigmatically related. Here is an example:

The	nurse teacher	disappeared. objected.
Arthur Harold Wilson	shot ridiculed	a man from the BBC. The Archbishop of Canterbury.

The items in each column are equivalent from the structural point of view and whichever is chosen will, when combined with items in the other columns, form a correct sentence. Thus *nurse* and *teacher* are equivalent but not *nurse* and *Harold Wilson*, the latter being equivalent to *The nurse*. Again, *disappeared* and *objected* are equivalent, appearing as they do in the same column, but they are not equivalent to *shot* or *ridiculed* but only to *shot the Archbishop of Canterbury* or *ridiculed a man from the BBC* since it is these verb phrases and not the verbs themselves which share the same column as the intransitive verb phrases.

What the substitution table makes clear is that a sentence is formed by *selecting* from items in a paradigmatic relationship and *combining* them with items from a different paradigmatic set. A sentence is both a selection and a combination and these two can be said to be the basic principles of linguistic organisation. But our discussion in the previous chapter of the language patterns created in literary discourse makes it clear that these patterns very commonly depend on a combination of items which are in paradigmatical relationship. That is to say, a selection is made of a series of items from the *same* column and equivalence is thereby transferred from the vertical plane of selection to the horizontal plane of combination. Thus, the lines quoted from Eliot's *Four Quartets* might be arranged into a substitution table as shown on the following page.

Such a table yields a number of paradigmatic choices which can be made to form a complete sentence: *Words strain under the burden, Words slip, Words decay with imprecision, Words will not stay still* and so on. What Eliot does, however, is to combine all the choices so that the linguistic elements become equivalent in combination as well as in selection, and the distinction between paradigmatic and syntagmatic relations is, as it were, neutralised in this context.

THE NATURE OF LITERARY COMMUNICATION

	strain crack break	under the burden. under the tension.
Words	slip. slide. perish. decay with imprecision. will not stay in place. will not stay still.	

The unique syntactic patterns of language created in literary discourse which, as was pointed out in the previous chapter, bestow a semantic value on the linguistic elements which constitute them, derive then from this transference of equivalence from selection to combination. As a further example, we can reduce some of the lines of Wordsworth which were previously discussed to the contents of a substitution table:

I	have felt	a presence	that disturbs me with the joy of elevated thoughts.	
		a sense sublime of something	far more deeply interfused.	
		a motion	whose dwelling is	the light of setting suns. the living air. the round ocean. the mind of man.
		a spirit	that impels	all thinking things. all objects of all thought.
			that rolls through all things.	

If we move from left to right selecting from each column we can construct a whole series of different sentences:

I have felt a presence that impels all thinking things.
I have felt a sense sublime of something that impels all objects of all thought.

I have felt a spirit far more deeply interfused.
I have felt a motion whose dwelling is the round ocean.
I have felt a spirit that disturbs me with the joy of elevated
thoughts.

Not only is each of these sentences a correct syntactic unit but each of them is semantically very similar to all the others. Any of them would serve as a passable summary of what the lines are about. Instead of selecting, however, Wordsworth combines all of the sentences into a pattern of equivalences and it is the fusion of the syntactic and semantic equivalence of these sentences which creates the particular effect of these lines: the effect (which was noticed in the previous chapter) of the poet trying to express the ineffable, trying to capture the essence of an experience which of its nature eludes a direct description. By organising Wordsworth's lines into a substitution table in this way we can show how paradigmatic and syntagmatic relations are combined to create a literary discourse. By so doing we can provide an account of the linguistic features of Wordsworth's style, the recognition of which underlies our impression of its 'sublimity', its 'grandeur' and so on. We can give linguistic support to the literary judgement. The use we have made of the substitution table in this discussion also points to a way it might be used in the teaching of literature.

We have considered aspects of a literary use of language which depend on a combination of what is kept distinct in the linguistic code. Let us now briefly review the converse: aspects of literary discourse which depend on dividing what is normally compounded. The most obvious instance of this, of course, is the separation of addresser from sender and addressee from receiver which has already been discussed at length earlier in this chapter. What has to be noticed is that this separation is symptomatic of the independence of literary discourse from the normal processes of social interaction and that it is because of this independence that internal patterns of language have to be designed within the discourse to carry meanings. These patterns are formed by reversing the normal principles of linguistic organisation. Thus, the dividing of what is combined leads to the combining of what is divided: the one is a consequence of the other. If the patterns of literary discourse were only conventional realisations of those of the language system the discourse would lose its independence and detachment and, in consequence, its literary character.

THE NATURE OF LITERARY COMMUNICATION

This is made clear in the poem of Roethke's which was discussed earlier in this chapter. The isolation of aspect from tense is the result of removing the discourse from any contact with previous interaction, but the consequence of this is that the occurrence of the continuous form of the verb cannot itself be isolated in the context: it has to pattern in with other instances. The first line of the poem:

The wind billowing out the seat of my britches . . .

makes no sense on its own (as it would if it were the reply to a question, or if it were linked with previous discourse in any other way). It only makes sense in association with the other lines of the poem, as part of a self-contained design. One might say, then, that the breaking of code patterns prepares the way for the creation of patterns in context.

The separation of what is normally combined is, then, symptomatic of the detachment of literary discourse. Other examples are provided by such opening lines as:

No, no, go not to Lethe, neither twist
Wolf's-bane, tight-rooted, for its poisonous wine . . .　　　(Keats)

Yes, I remember Adlestrop . . .　　　(Edward Thomas)

These are replies to questions that have never been put. In normal circumstances one just cannot initiate a discourse in this way since an answer must be dependent on a question previously posed. These lines make no sense on their own. They only make sense in association with the rest of the poem in which they appear: being cut off from one link they have to form others.

At this point another pervasive peculiarity of literary discourse comes up for consideration, and one which illustrates once more the way in which conventional distinctions are effaced in literature. The two quotations cited above sound like *spoken* replies, one catches the cadence of the speaking voice; but at the same time the lines are of course cast in the medium of the *written* form. Furthermore the careful organisation of language in the poems which develop from these first lines suggest a written mode of communicating. The actual physical channel, the *medium*, used in literature is (in most cases) that of writing but the *mode* of communication is commonly not that which is conventionally associated with that medium. Consider poetry, for example: the patterning of sound and stress upon which poetic meanings so often depend are obviously intended to appeal to the ear, and in this respect poetry has the character of communication in the spoken mode. But the very effort that goes into achieving these and other effects, the painstaking composition, the revising and rewriting, all of this is normally associated with the written and not the spoken mode. The medium is writing, but the mode of communicating is not definitely spoken or written in a conventional sense but a blend of both. Other forms of literature reveal a similar ambiguous amalgam of spoken and written. Literature, as we shall see again presently when we look at certain features of short stories, appears to be a mode of communicating which has no analogue in conventional uses of language.

I have talked at some length already of the use of pronouns in literary writing and I have pointed out that the first person has an internal reference to some entity in the discourse itself and not an external reference to the sender. The question arises: what does the third person pronoun refer to? It is very common to find literary works beginning with a third person pronoun for which there is no previous reference. In normal circumstances, if one uses 'he' or 'she', for example, these pronouns refer to someone previously mentioned or someone in the immediate situation of utterance (that is to say, with reference to terms discussed in Chapter 2, the pronoun is either anaphoric or deictic). 'He' and 'she' stand for known human referents. In literary writing, however, this is commonly not the case. Consider the following examples:

> She walks in beauty like the night . . .   (Byron)

> She was a phantom of delight . . .   (Wordsworth)

Who is this 'she'? In neither of these poems are we ever told. The pronoun takes on the character of a Proper noun: it operates as an independent reference in a way in which it never operates in normal discourse.

Fiction provides innumerable instances of the use of third person pronouns which have no antecedent reference: The following, for example, are all short story openings:*

> He came back into the kitchen. The man was still on the floor, lying where he had hit him, and his face was bloody . . .
> (Somerset Maugham: *The Unconquered*)

* I have deliberately drawn most of my illustrations from the following books on the assumption that they should be fairly easily accessible to readers wishing to follow up the points I raise and to subject the stories referred to to closer investigation: Christopher Dolley (ed.), *The Penguin Book of English Short Stories*; James Cochrane (ed.), *The Penguin Book of American Short Stories*.

She was sitting on the verandah waiting for her husband to come in
for luncheon.   (Somerset Maugham: *The Force of Circumstance*)

Flame-lurid his face as he turned among the throng of flame-lit and
dark faces upon the platform. In the light of the furnace she caught
sight of his drifting countenance.
(D. H. Lawrence: *Fanny and Annie*)

Soon now they would enter the Delta. The sensation was familiar
to him.   (William Faulkner: *Delta Autumn*)

It was an eighty-cow dairy, and the troop of milkers, regular and
supernumerary, were all at work.   (Hardy: *The Withered Arm*)

Since there is no preceding discourse to which these sentences can
relate, the pronouns have no reference and the reader takes them,
as it were, on trust. Unlike the pronouns in the lines from the poems
which were cited above, however, they do take on referential value
from the discourse that follows. As the story progresses we learn
who is being referred to. Whereas in ordinary discourse, then, pronouns derive their value *retrospectively* from what has preceded, in
literary discourse it is common for them to derive their value
prospectively from what follows. Again, it is the discourse itself which
provides for the deficiency in meaning which arises from the isolation
of the discourse from any wider context.

It frequently happens, then, that in literary discourse the third
person pronouns are not anaphoric in function but (with reference
to the distinctions made in Chapter 2) operate in a way which we
might describe as homophoric or deictic, as in the case of the lines
from Byron and Wordsworth, or cataphoric, as in the case of the
short story openings. These pronouns do not normally function in
this way. The distinctions between anaphora, cataphora and homo-
phora were made by Halliday and recorded in Chapter 2 in connection with the definite article and all of the prose extracts quoted
above contain noun phrases with definite articles which, if we use
structural criteria ought to be either anaphoric or deictic. Their
function cannot be anaphoric, however, since there is nothing for
these phrases to refer back to: *The man was still on the floor*—
which man? We have not been told. On the other hand, the reference
cannot be deictic either in any normal way since we are not present
in the kitchen referred to and we do not see the man on the floor.
But although we do not know, and cannot know, the identity of the
man and are not physically present in the situation described, the
absence of any possible previous mention and the absence of the
features which usually signal cataphoric reference in effect inclines

us to interpret these definite noun phrases deictically. That is to say, the effect of the use of phrases like *The man* and the pronoun *he* and *she* without previous mention is to draw the reader into the imagined situation and to provide an immediacy of reference by involving the reader as a participant in the situation itself. Of course, as we read on we are provided with the information necessary to give specificity to these references and in this respect we can regard them as cataphoric in function, the information being transferred from its normal place in the noun phrase to later parts of the discourse. We may conclude, then, that in their initial effect the definite noun phrases and the pronouns in these extracts function deictically and provide the reader with a sort of immediacy of involvement but that at the same time the reader treats them as incomplete cataphoric reference and reads on to discover the required information. Thus the reader is both involved in the present and projected into the future. Once again we see how functions combine in literary discourse.

The purpose of throwing the reference forward, of projecting the reader's attention towards what is to come, is of course precisely to make us read on: to set up expectations in the reader other than those he naturally brings to his reading by virtue of his knowledge of the language code and the way it is normally used. As has already been pointed out, the literary writer uses language in such a way as to make the reader anticipate what is to come and the use of definite noun phrases to project the reader forward rather than to refer him back is an instance of this.

Here are other examples of the dual functioning of definite reference:

> The Picton boat was due to leave at half past eleven.
> (Katherine Mansfield: *The Voyage*)

> The room was warm and clean, the curtains drawn, the two table lamps alight . . . (Raold Dahl: *Lamb to the Slaughter*)

> The lieutenant stood in front of the steel sphere and gnawed a piece of pine splinter. (H. G. Wells: *In the Abyss*)

> There were two white men in charge of the trading station.
> (Conrad: *An Outpost of Progress*)

The occurrence of aspect without tense and of pronouns and definite noun phrases which normally presuppose previous mention or a referent situationally present but which have no antecedent reference in the context or direct reference in the situation are both features of language use which reflect the independence of literary discourse.

In both cases their value derives from their association with other linguistic features within the discourse itself.

This independence, on which I have laid such stress, has another consequence which might be mentioned and which has to do with the ambiguity of literature as a mode of communication which has already been referred to in connection with poetry. In conventional discourse it is not generally necessary to provide details about the participants and the setting in terms of time and place. If the discourse is spoken most of these details appear within the actual situation and those which do not emerge in the course of the interaction are irrelevant. In written discourse facts about the sender/addresser as a person (as opposed to a persona acting out a role) are only relevant in personal correspondence and in this case they are known. Facts about the time and place in which the sending actually occurs are generally irrelevant since it is of the nature of written language to be dissociated from an immediate situation shared by both participants. Where the discourse is removed from a social context, however, and where the sender is no longer to be identified with the addresser, nor the receiver with the addressee, the situation in which the interaction takes place has to be created. The facts about the participants and about the setting in which they interact have to be included within the discourse itself. In consequence, its mode of communicating is really neither spoken nor written in any straightforward way but a combination of both.

It is for this reason that prose fiction is marked by frequent descriptions of persons and settings: they represent the necessary situational context within which the actions, including the verbal actions, of the participants can be understood. In short stories it is common to find information of this kind introduced at the beginning, as in the quotation from Dahl. The opening from Conrad's *An Outpost of Progress* which was also quoted earlier continues as follows:

> There were two white men in charge of the trading station. Kayerts, the chief, was short and fat; Carlier, the assistant, was tall, with a large head and a very broad trunk perched upon a long pair of thin legs.

The following are two further examples of openings:

> Day had broken cold and gray, exceedingly cold and gray, when the man turned aside from the main Yukon trail and climbed the high earth-bank, where a dim and little-travelled trail led eastward through the fat spruce timberland.   (Jack London: *To Build a Fire*)

> It was the dead hour of a November afternoon. Under the ceiling of level mud-coloured cloud, the latest office buildings of the city stood out alarmingly like new tombstones among the mass of older buildings.   (V. S. Pritchett: *The Fly in the Ointment*)

The account of persons and settings is not, however, a straight-forward one (as, indeed, we might not expect it to be). As the situation is one which is removed from the reality of normal social life there is no need to keep the different situational factors distinct. Again we see the combining principle at work. Thus it is common to find that instead of having persons, times and places described as separate aspects of the situation they are interrelated as features of a kind of composite reality which we usually refer to as the 'theme'. Consider again, for example, the opening of Lawrence's story *Fanny and Annie*:

> Flame-lurid his face as he turned among the throng of flame-lit and dark faces upon the platform. In the light of the furnace she caught sight of his drifting countenance, like a piece of floating fire. And the nostalgia, the doom of homecoming went through her veins like a drug. His eternal face, flame-lit now! The pulse and darkness of red fire from the furnace towers in the sky, lighting the desultory, industrial crowd on the wayside station, lit him and went out.
> Of course he did not see her. Flame-lit and unseeing! . . .

The scene here, the darkness and the red light from the furnace, is inextricably involved with the man's appearance. The light is both an external phenomenon, a feature of the place, and a reflection of some inner quality of the man; it is both *on* his face and *in* his face. The person and the place are represented in terms of each other. This is the reality which Fanny sees as the addresser, for it is her impressions which are recorded and which constitute the underlying theme of the story. The third person pronoun is used but, as we have already discovered, this pronoun can (and does here) take on additional first person features. A glance at this passage from *Fanny and Annie* makes it clear that the pronouns *he his him* have a very different value from *she her*—the former have no first person overtones whereas the latter do.

The kind of description of person and setting which is required in literary discourse has no exact analogue in other uses of language. We have already seen how person and setting can be blended together (and the example from Lawrence is by no means an isolated one) but even when personal description is not involved with setting there is a combination of features which characterises it as literary. Conventionally, for example, we can have a description of appearance (as might be recorded by a police witness) or a description of character (as might be recorded in a personal reference) but literary descriptions tend to combine the two. Consider this example:

> He was a little man, considerably less than of middle height, and enormously stout; he had a large, fleshy face, clean-shaven, with the cheeks hanging on each side in great dewlaps, and three vast chins; his small features were all dissolved in fat; and, but for a crescent of white hair at the back of his head, he was completely bald. He reminded you of Mr. Pickwick. He was grotesque, a figure of fun, and yet, strangely enough, not without dignity. His blue eyes, behind large gold-rimmed spectacles, were shrewd and vivacious, and there was a great deal of determination in his face. He was sixty, but his native vitality triumphed over advancing years. Notwithstanding his corpulence his movements were quick, and he walked with a heavy, resolute tread as though he sought to impress his weight upon the earth. He spoke in a loud, gruff voice.
>
> (Somerset Maugham: *Mackintosh*)

Here the man's physical appearance and his personality are described in terms of each other: his eyes are blue and shrewd, his face is fleshy and determined, his tread is heavy and resolute. As in the extract from Forster's *A Passage to India* which was considered in the previous chapter, details which would normally be appropriate to different kinds of description are represented as features of the same thing and they take on a unique value accordingly. I shall be considering this passage from Somerset Maugham more closely in Chapter 6.

Let me summarise the main points that have been made in this chapter. Literary discourse is dissociated from an immediate social context and its meaning has to be self-contained. What the writer has to say cannot of its nature be conveyed by conventional means and in consequence he has to devise his own fashion of communicating. This consists essentially in reversing the normal principles of language structure and use, combining what is normally distinct and making distinct what is normally combined. The result of this is that our conventional concept of reality, realised as it is through the language code and the standard uses we make of it, is disturbed. It is still recognisably the reality with which we are familiar, just as the language in literary discourse is recognisably that which we use in our everyday affairs, but turned, as it were, inside out—a reality which is presented in a strange new perspective:

> . . . both a new world
> And the old made explicit.   (Eliot: Burnt Norton*)

* T. S. Eliot, *Four Quartets* (Burnt Norton), Faber and Faber, 1959.

But the explicitness is never complete: the reality which underlies that which is conventionally accepted is an elusive one, its various and changing facets reflected only through an individual vision. The literary writer captures his perception of this reality in the way he manipulates language but the patterns that he creates express also the very elusiveness of what he perceives. If it were not elusive, if it could be brought within the compass of what is conventionally communicable, then of course it would be incorporated into the structure of normal social attitudes and beliefs, and would thereby be falsified. So the patterns of language which the literary writer designs must both capture a unique experience and express the elusiveness which is an intrinsic feature of it: they must not be so regular as to be predictable. It is for this reason that, in reading the lines of Wordsworth's *Tintern Abbey* and the passages from Lawrence previously discussed, for example, the reader is kept in suspense as to how the language patterns will develop.

What literature communicates, then, is an individual awareness of a reality other than that which is given general social sanction but nevertheless related to it. Of its nature unstable, incomplete, kaleidoscopic, it cannot be described but only expressed. The reader of literature has his expectations aroused by the patterns of language which give shape to the writer's perception of this other reality and then experiences its elusiveness as these expectations are denied when the patterns change. An understanding of what literature communicates necessarily involves an understanding of how it communicates: what and how are not distinct. It is for this reason that literary works cannot be satisfactorily paraphrased or explained by any single interpretation: to do so is to recast their essential ambiguity into the definite shape of conventional statement. The basic problem in the teaching of literature is to develop in the student an awareness of the what/how of literary communication and this can only be done by relating it to, without translating it into, normal uses of language. It is at this point that we turn to pedagogic questions.

PART TWO

5

Literature as subject
and discipline

The preceding chapters have presented an approach to the study of
literature which is stylistic in the sense defined in Chapter 1 in that it
attempts to characterise literary writing as discourse and so to mediate
between the linguist's treatment of literature primarily as text and the
critic's treatment of it primarily as messages. Such an approach seeks
to show how the use of linguistic patterns creates a form of communication which conveys the unique reality of the individual vision.
In Chapter 1 I made the claim that an approach of this kind is of
particular value for the study of literature as a subject. My purpose
in this and the succeeding chapter is to substantiate this claim. In
the present chapter I shall try to show how the approach that has
been described can indicate how the subject of literary studies might
be defined and in the chapter that follows I shall discuss a number
of ways in which the subject might actually be taught in the classroom. This chapter, then, is concerned with certain pedagogical
principles and the next with some of the pedagogical practices which
might realise them.

It might of course be objected that there is no need to define
literary studies as a subject by reference to stylistics since teachers
already have a clear enough idea as to what the aims and procedures
of a literature course should be, even though these might not have
been defined in terms of explicit principles. There are two points
to be made here, I think. The first is that although individual teachers
may often work out a way of teaching literature as a subject, their
own experience as students and the type of examination for which
they must prepare their pupils will tend to make them define literature
as a subject with reference only to literature as a discipline. The
teacher and examiner of literature will take his cue from the literary
scholar just as the teacher and examiner of language will take his
cue from the linguist, the assumption being that in each case the
subject is a simplified and abridged version of the discipline to which

it is most obviously related. This is not surprising since it is still generally true to say that the teacher of language and literature has no training other than what he might acquire incidentally in studying for his first degree, so that his only guide as to what and how to teach to others is what and how he was taught himself and first degree courses are (again, generally speaking) discipline-based.

The first point, then, is that the teacher's idea of what a literature course should be is likely, in the absence of other guidance, to derive directly from his knowledge of literature as a discipline. Of course, experience in teaching might well, in time, indicate how the discipline should be modified to suit a particular pedagogic purpose and this brings us to the second point. There is a good deal of evidence in the form of papers at conferences and articles in journals that many teachers are actively engaged in working out what the aims and procedures of literature teaching should be. What seems to be lacking, however, is an explicit set of principles to which different aims and procedures can be related and which might serve to define the subject. Unless individual ideas can be related to a more general scheme of thinking, the danger is that these ideas, though effective for the person who propounds them, cannot be adapted to suit different circumstances. Adaptation can only be made with reference to underlying principles.

It seems to me, then, that what is needed is an explicit and pedago-gically oriented definition of the nature of literary study as a subject, one which specifies aims in terms of educational objectives, and actual teaching procedures in terms of these aims. As was pointed out in Chapter 1, these objectives will vary according to different levels of education: the higher the level, the closer will the subject come to resemble the discipline. Some pupils will become students and some students will become scholars, and one can say that this process is one of gradual approximation of literature as subject to literature as discipline. These objectives will also vary, of course, according to whether the literature being taught is that of the first or of a second or foreign language.

Let us first consider how we might define literature as a subject in general. We may begin with a quotation from F. R. Leavis which indicates what the author sees as the essential benefits deriving from a study of literature, and in particular from a study of English literature:

> The essential discipline of an English School is the literary-critical;
> it is a true discipline, only in an English School if anywhere will it

be fostered, and it is irreplaceable. It trains, in a way no other discipline can, intelligence and sensibility together, cultivating sensitiveness and precision of response and a delicate integrity of intelligence—intelligence that integrates as well as analyzes and must have pertinacity and staying power as well as delicacy . . . There is no need to add at the moment, by way of indicating the inherent educational possibilities of the literary-critical discipline, than that it can, in its peculiar preoccupation with the concrete, provide an incomparably inward and subtle initiation into the nature and significance of tradition.*

Now it might be thought that here we have a statement of the aims of a literature course which can serve as a basic definition of our subject: to train intelligence and sensibility, to cultivate sensitiveness and precision of response, to provide an initiation into the nature and significance of tradition. But there are difficulties.

In the first place, these supposed effects of a literary-critical discipline are of an extremely general and idealistic kind. Leavis's remarks here resemble propaganda rather than a reasoned set of proposals and it is difficult to see how, as they stand, they could possibly serve as a guide to how a literature course might be designed. This is not to say that the effects that Leavis ascribes to literary study may not be achieved, nor that one should not frame a literature course in the belief that such effects should ultimately be brought about. But pedagogic aims have to be more limited and realistic and within the scope of reasonable attainment. What Leavis says here serves to stimulate ideas about the philosophy of literary study as a discipline but it gives little or no indication as to how one might define the pedagogy of literary study as a subject.

A second difficulty in the way of accepting this statement as a basis for the definition of the aims of a literature course, at any educational level, is that there are a number of other disciplines which might justifiably claim to train people to acquire precision of response, awareness of the significance of tradition and so on. Leavis, not unnaturally, believes that literary studies provide this kind of training more effectively than do studies of other kinds but in the absence of any evidence there is no reason for accepting such a belief. Scholars whose allegiance is to other disciplines, like History, Sociology, and the different branches of the Physical Sciences, could all make the sort of claim that Leavis makes. Indeed, one might

* F. R. Leavis, *Education and the University*, Chatto & Windus, 1943, pp. 34–35.

say that what he has described is the desirable effect of all education no matter what particular speciality is involved.

Now if it is the case that the kind of effects that Leavis describes can also be legitimately associated with other areas of enquiry, the question arises as to what it is that characterises literary studies as distinct from these other areas. And here we come to the most striking deficiency in Leavis's statement taken as a definition of literary studies either as subject or discipline: no mention is made of language. Now, whatever benefits are received through a study of literature, the means whereby these benefits are bestowed must relate in some measure to an awareness of the subtleties of language use. There is a sense in which other areas of study have a conceptual content which can be distinguished from a particular manner of expressing it but, as the previous chapters have demonstrated, the concepts of literature are in essence indistinguishable from their verbal expression. A summary abstract of a scientific paper retains the character of scientific statement, but a summary of a poem or a novel ceases to be literature. So it would seem evident that however one wishes to define the discipline of literary studies one must find room somewhere in the definition for those features of the discipline which distinguish it from others. The most obvious distinguishing feature is not that literary study can have the kind of beneficial effects that Leavis describes, since such effects can be achieved through a study of other disciplines, but that these effects come about through a heightened awareness of the way language can be used to explore and express realities other than that which is communally accepted as the most socially convenient. It is true that a study of literature requires sensitivity, intelligence, precision of response and so on because it takes the reader into unknown territory where familiar signs may be few and where he must often find his own way by following recondite clues. But the signs and clues are linguistic, the sensitivity must initially be a sensitivity to language and the intelligence and precision of response can only be developed as general qualities through literature if they are first shaped by practice in interpreting the unique language use of literary discourse.

It might be argued, of course, that Leavis is talking about literary studies in British universities and that he assumes that students will already have acquired a fair degree of linguistic sensitivity. But the point is that literary studies have not generally been defined as a subject in such a way as to develop such a sensitivity, either in secondary schools or in universities. What tends to be taught is some critical orthodoxy, a set of ready-made judgements for rote-learning rather than strategies of understanding which can be transferred to other and unknown literary works. Instead of being guided towards techniques of individual interpretation students are often provided with other people's interpretations so that the study of literature becomes identified with the study of literary criticism and commentary. This is what C. S. Lewis has to say on the matter:

> Everyone who sees the work of Honours students of English at a university has noticed with distress their increasing tendency to see books wholly through the spectacles of other books. On every play, poem or novel, they produce the view of some eminent critic. An amazing knowledge of Chaucerian or Shakespearean criticism sometimes co-exists with a very inadequate knowledge of Chaucer or Shakespeare. Less and less do we meet the individual response. The all-important conjunction (Reader meets Text) never seems to have been allowed to occur of itself and develop spontaneously. Here, plainly, are young people drenched, dizzied, and bedevilled by criticism to a point at which primary literary experience is no longer possible.*

There is a suggestion here (if I interpret Lewis correctly) that the individual response arises naturally from exposure to literature and can develop spontaneously. I would argue that, in most cases, the individual can only respond to literature as a result of guidance. The conjunction Reader Meets Text very often simply produces bafflement: one cannot just expose students to literary writing and hope that they will be apprised of its essential message by some kind of miraculous revelation. What critics and teachers so often do is to tell students what messages are to be found in the literary works they are studying and this, as Lewis observes, discourages them from seeking out messages for themselves. But as has been pointed out in previous chapters, the literary message is integrated within the discourse, and when it is separated out it is inevitably reduced to conventional terms. It follows that the meaning of a literary work, intrinsic as it is to the unique use of language, can only be recognised by the individual because once it is expressed in different terms so as to be communicated to others it must inevitably change. This does not mean that what teachers and critics say about a literary work may not reveal a good deal of its meaning but only that the full import of the work can only be recognised by the individual's direct experience of it. This recognition by experience will not, however,

* C. S. Lewis, *An Experiment in Criticism*, Oxford University Press, 1961, pp. 128–129.

occur spontaneously by simple exposure: although there are people who acquire an understanding and appreciation of literature by intuition most of us need guidance as to what to look for. And it is precisely to provide such guidance that we require a subject of literary study.

I would argue, then, that the benefits that Leavis associates with literary studies can only be realised if the student develops an awareness of the way language is used in literary discourse for the conveying of unique messages, and I would suggest that it is the purpose of literary study as a subject to further this development. Put another way, literature as a subject has as its principal aim the development of the capacity for individual response to language use. Before going on to discuss how this aim might be achieved, however, mention should be made of the situation where the literature being taught is not that of the mother tongue, and in particular where English literature is taught overseas to students whose mother tongue is not English.

As has been pointed out, Leavis's remarks are made with British universities in mind—or at least with universities in English-speaking countries in mind (and we must not forget that the remarks were made over 30 years ago). I have suggested a number of reasons why these remarks are unsatisfactory in general as a basis for defining English literature as a subject and I have been thinking primarily of English-speaking education. When one considers the teaching of English literature in situations where English is the foreign or second language Leavis's remarks become even more open to objection. The reason for this is not hard to see: it is that all of the beneficial effects that Leavis associates with what he calls 'the literary-critical discipline' could equally well derive from a study of the native language literature so that what Leavis has to say has no relevance at all to the establishing of *English* literature as a subject for study in non-English speaking countries. If it is the proper study of literature in general that promotes qualities like sensitivity, precision of response and so on (and it is hard to see how one could argue that it is only the study of English literature in particular which can do so) then it presumably does not matter whether one studies Italian, French, German, Russian, Arabic or any other literature. Leavis here provides no justification whatever for studying a foreign literature in countries which already have a literature of their own, nor, if a case *can* be made out for teaching a foreign literature, why this literature should be in English.

One might, of course, take a chauvinistic line and claim that English literature is the best in the world so that the beneficial effects of studying it are likely to be correspondingly greater than those gained from reading an 'inferior' literature. This view, indefensible though it might be, is by no means uncommon (and by no means restricted, incidentally, to native English speakers). Such a view, or something resembling it, would appear to underlie the following remarks by John Holloway:

> Needless to say, students of English literature, wherever they are, can be expected to draw from their studies the benefits of 'English' as a broad, flexible, and liberal discipline, concerned with a literature which is not clearly excelled by any other, either in quality or continuity over a long period of time . . . There is no systematic study of literature which does not foster many qualities of mind—judgement (both intellectual and moral); cogency and flexibility of mind; maturity of understanding; and a sense of evidence, of detail, and of history being among them.*

These remarks are made in very much the same spirit as those of Leavis and are open to the same objections. One notices how the discussion shifts from English literature to literature, the implication being that it is English literature which has the particular power to foster the qualities of mind which are mentioned. But a case for the systematic study of literature is one thing and the case for the systematic study of *English* literature is another. All the benefits that Leavis and Holloway believe accrue from a study of literature must surely derive from a study of any literature and not just that in English. There must therefore be other reasons for promoting the study of English literature in particular.

If one rejects the argument that English literature should be taught because it is the best and so the most likely to foster desirable qualities of mind, one seems to be left with two other possible reasons for teaching it overseas. These reasons relate to the two ways of interpreting the term 'English literature'. One may interpret it as meaning the literature of England including (by courtesy) Ireland, Scotland and Wales and perhaps even the English-speaking countries of North America and the Antipodes. The reason for teaching English literature in this sense would be essentially a cultural one: to acquaint students with ways of looking at the world which characterise the cultures of the English-speaking peoples. To

---

* John Holloway, *Aspects of the study of English Literature in Afro-Asian Countries*, in John Press (ed.), pp. 20–21.

teach English literature as a cultural subject is to adopt perspectives usually associated with History, Sociology and Social Anthropology. It is presumably the cultural aspect of literature that Leavis refers to when he speaks of it providing an 'initiation into the nature and significance of tradition' and that Holloway refers to when he mentions a sense of history as being among the qualities of mind that literary study fosters. The second way of interpreting the term 'English literature' is to gloss it as 'literature written in the English language'. On this interpretation, the reason for teaching it would be essentially a linguistic one. I mean by this that its basic purpose would be to acquaint students with the manner in which literary works in English use the language to convey special meanings. I am using the term 'linguistic', therefore, to refer to discourse as well as text as I have defined these notions in the preceding chapters. To teach English literature in this sense as a linguistic subject is of course to adopt a stylistics perspective.

A case can be made out (and often is made out) for the teaching of English literature as a cultural subject overseas. One difficulty, however, is that unless it is integrated with a linguistic approach (and I shall return presently to how the two approaches might be related) literary works tend to be studied not for themselves but as evidence for something else: they take on the character of historical or sociological documentation. As such, the nature of literary writing as discourse, in the sense previously defined, is practically irrelevant. If literature is studied for an exclusively cultural purpose there seems little reason why it should not be studied in translation and indeed in classrooms where the cultural purpose is paramount translation is a very common teaching technique: the 'main points' of the work being studied are extracted and transferred into the mother tongue.

The difficulty about the treatment of literature as a cultural subject, then, is that the literature tends to become simply a repository of factual data. This kind of treatment is not, of course, restricted to overseas teaching: indeed it is the traditional way of dealing with literature in British secondary schools. Such an approach regards a poem or a play or a novel as a source of information like any other source of information and it directs the learners' attention to questions of the following kind:

What did A look like?
What kind of person was B?
What happened when A met B at X?

Who did A meet at X and what did they talk about?
What does Shelley compare the West Wind with?
What does 'Tintern Abbey' tell us about Wordsworth's philosophy?
What do we learn about Victorian London by reading 'Oliver Twist'?

and so on.

The point about questions of this sort is that they reduce literature to the level of conventional statement about ordinary reality. The questions about people and events could equally well be asked about actual people and events in past or present real life situations and the distinction between fact and fiction, the real and the imagined world, disappears. Again, the question about Wordsworth is no different from a question like 'What does the second chapter of "An Essay concerning Human Understanding" tell us about Locke's philosophy?' and the question about 'Oliver Twist' could equally well be asked with reference to Mayhew's 'The Great World of London' or any number of contemporary documents on Victorian urban life. Questions such as these, then, are not directed at the specifically literary nature of literature: instead they treat literature as a source of information such as we might treat conventional forms of discourse like a historical document, a philosophical treatise, a sociological questionnaire.

The cultural approach leads to a treatment of literature as a source of facts. It might be worth pointing out, in passing, that it also tends to lead to a conception of literature as a chronological sequence. Most literature courses at universities begin in the distant past (Beowulf, Chaucer and Shakespeare being favourite starting points) and advance towards the present through every major 'period' on the way, usually stopping well short of writing which could reasonably be regarded as contemporary. So what students gain from such an approach is not an insight into the beliefs, values and so on of contemporary English-speaking societies but a knowledge of their past culture, and what is sometimes referred to as their 'cultural heritage'.

There are no doubt good reasons why in some situations—both where the literature is in the mother tongue and where it is not— it is justifiable to use literature rather than other forms of discourse to train students to extract relevant facts from a mass of data or to use it to teach social and cultural history. Two points must be borne in mind, however. Firstly, as has been implied, this ability and this knowledge might after all best be taught by using material other than literature. The second point is that by using literature in this way one is inevitably misrepresenting its essential nature so that whatever else one may be doing one is not teaching literature as such: one is using literature to teach something else. Thus one cannot base a definition of literature as a subject solely on cultural criteria.

Whether one attempts to associate literary study with some kind of intellectual or moral effect or with the transmission of cultural knowledge of some kind one comes up with the difficulty that in neither case is there an appeal made to the particular character of literature itself. Other disciplines provide an opportunity for intellectual and moral development so we clearly cannot define the discipline of literary studies in these terms. Similarly, an acquisition of cultural knowledge and the ability to process data so as to arrive at the relevant facts can both be brought about by other than literary means. Indeed, the use of literary means involves a misrepresentation of the real nature of literature.

In view of these difficulties, let us then consider whether it would not be better to define literary studies as a linguistic subject in the sense in which I have defined that term: an enquiry into the way a language is used to express a reality other than that expressed by conventional means. What this amounts to, of course, is the study of literary works as kinds of discourse. If one defines the subject in this way, the reason for teaching it overseas becomes immediately apparent. Pupils and students are engaged in learning the English language: this involves in part a learning of the language system—the structures and vocabulary of English—but it must involve also the learning of how this system is used in the actual business of communication. This being so, the manner in which the resources of the language system are used in the fashioning of unique literary messages can be compared with other uses of the language so as to make clear by contrast how the system is used in conventional forms of communication. At the same time, of course, a comparison with other kinds of discourse will reveal what it is that is peculiar to literary uses of English.

What I would suggest is that stylistics, as discussed in the preceding chapters, provides a way of integrating the two subjects, English language and English literature, which are commonly taught in isolation one from the other. The unfortunate consequences of such a separation have often been noted. It is not unusual to find literature teachers, both in first and second language situations, attempting to teach literary 'classics' (presumably for either moral or cultural reasons or both) to learners whose knowledge of the system and use of English is so limited as to make the work being presented to them almost totally incomprehensible. Very often the teacher resorts to translation and paraphrase to overcome linguistic difficulties. Such a procedure not only has the effect of misrepresenting the nature of literature (as has already been pointed out) but also of creating a resistance to it in the learner's mind. For, if a writer's meaning can be expressed in simpler terms, then why, the learner will reasonably ask, does he choose to express himself in such an unnecessarily complex way? Literature takes on the character in the learner's mind of a mysterious and perversely roundabout way of saying something that could be said much more simply and directly in another way.

If literature as a subject is given a stylistic basis, however, the selection of works to be taught will inevitably be controlled by the learner's capacity to understand the language which is used. Furthermore, if the teaching of language and literature are regarded as aspects of the same activity, then this will require the language teacher to develop materials for the teaching of use to complement those he uses for the teaching of system. To put the matter simply: if literature is to be taught as a form of discourse then on the one hand its textual features must be such as to relate to what the learner knows of English grammar and vocabulary and on the other hand he must be introduced to other forms of discourse, of a conventional type, with which the literary discourse can be compared. Notice that this comparison yields reciprocal benefits: the uniqueness of literary discourse is revealed by relating it to conventional forms of language use and this in turn involves the study of how language is used conventionally in other forms of discourse. Thus the learning of the language system is extended into the learning of language use.

If one defines the subject of literature in these terms it can provide both for those students whose education will stop short well before they encounter the principles of literary study as a discipline and for those who will take up literary study as an advanced speciality. It will not only develop in students an awareness of the communicative potential of the language they are learning, which can be brought to bear on their further experience of both conventional and literary discourse in that language (thus fulfilling an educational purpose of providing a basis for further learning without specific instruction), but it will also serve as a basis for further studies where learning takes place in the context of formal education. In other words, I would claim that if literary studies are conceived of in this way they meet the two requirements of a school or university subject: on the one hand they provide something of educational value for the learners who will not be going on to more advanced study and on the other hand they provide a basis for those who will. Furthermore, a stylistics approach to literature must of its very nature relate linguistic and literary perspectives so that it can serve as a preparation both for those whose later studies will move towards the discipline of linguistics and for those who will move towards that of literary criticism.

I would argue that the linguistic approach to literary studies deriving from the kind of stylistic analysis demonstrated in the preceding chapters allows for the 'systematic teaching of literature' which Holloway refers to but does not exemplify. At the same time, it does not preclude the adoption of the other aims of literature teaching which we have considered: on the contrary it provides the means whereby, if desirable, these other aims can be achieved. Once the learner has acquired an awareness of how literary discourse works then he may go on to recognise its cultural and moral implications. But it is difficult to see how these loftier aims can be attained otherwise. It is not uncommon to find teachers in both an English-speaking and a non-English-speaking context attempting to achieve these 'higher' aims directly and succeeding only in mystifying their pupils and students, who have no way of linking the concepts and aesthetic effects being talked about with their own experience of language. It is not surprising that there is so often so little participation in literature classes and that there is so much boredom and resentment in consequence. To adopt a linguistic approach to literature, then, is not to prevent the acquisition of benefits of a cultural or moral kind but on the contrary to provide for their promotion in a systematic way. And even if these benefits are not acquired, the learner will have acquired others of practical educational value. To adopt the loftier cultural and moral purpose as a basis for defining the subject of literary studies, however, is to run the risk of representing literature as something arcane, pretentious and irrelevant.

The point about relevance is a crucial one. Any subject must engage the interest and ensure the participation of pupils or students.

It will not do so, however, unless the pupils/students feel that what they are being taught is relevant to their present concerns and to their future needs. What this very often means in effect is that literature must be shown to contribute to the learning of something useful. The approach that has been proposed demonstrates the usefulness of literature by showing how it can develop a sharper awareness of the communicative resources of the language being learned. It can help in the acquisition of essential skills of communication by extending the study of system to the practice of putting it to use in both the comprehension and the production of different kinds of discourse necessary for the learner's further education or his work. Let me stress again, however, that this practical justification for the study of literature does not entail a rejection of the cultural and moral aims but only a recognition that these 'higher' and more abstract aims can only be reached through the more practical systematic study that is allowed for by the stylistically based definition of literature as a subject.

Let us now consider some of the basic pedagogic principles that follow from the kind of stylistic approach to literary study that has been outlined in this book. Firstly, the study of literature is primarily a study of language use and as such it is not a separate activity from language learning but an aspect of the same activity. Secondly, it follows that the study of literature is an overtly comparative one, since not otherwise can it be practised as an aspect of language learning in a more general sense. This principle can be put into practice by considering examples of literary discourse alongside conventional uses of language to demonstrate the differences in the way the language system is realised for communicative purposes. The assumption is that this comparative procedure will develop in the learner two kinds of ability. The first is the ability to recognise the manner in which the signification of linguistic elements is modified by context and thereby to acquire a strategy for ascertaining their value in actual use. Since it is common to find considerable divergence between signification and value in literary discourse, most obviously in the use of metaphor, literature can be used to demonstrate the kind of reasoning process which must operate in the understanding of any discourse. The argument is that understanding literature and understanding other kinds of discourse involve the same correlating procedure of matching code and context meanings but in understanding literary discourse the procedure is made more overt and self-conscious.

The first kind of ability, then, has to do with the relating of the language system to the way it is used in communication in general. The second has to do with the relating of different kinds of use. The assumption in this case is that a careful investigation into how messages are communicated in literary discourse is bound to bring into the open the way messages are communicated in conventional discourse. Thus, for example, an understanding of how pronouns take on unique values in literary writing clearly depends on an understanding of how pronouns operate normally, so that setting a literary use alongside a non-literary one will inevitably lead to a consideration of how conventional communication operates and in what respect it differs from literary discourse. The same point can be made in relation to all the other deviant features of language use which were discussed in the preceding chapters. All literary appreciation is comparative, as indeed is a recognition of styles in general, and what we are doing here is simply establishing a covert intuitive practice as an overt pedagogic principle. In this way we hope to give systematic attention to what would otherwise be vague and inconsistent and so to provide learners with an opportunity to develop what Leavis calls 'precision of response'. For those who have no immediate response at all, except perhaps puzzlement, overt comparison can yield definite evidence upon which a response of some sort can be made.

One final point should be made about the teaching of literature along the lines that have been suggested here: it is concerned not with the transmission of facts and ready-made interpretations but with the development in the learners of interpretative procedures which can be applied to a range of language uses, both literary and non-literary, which they encounter inside and outside the formal learning situation. The purpose of literature as a subject, as it has been defined in this chapter, is not to provide information about the particular pieces of literature in the syllabus but to get the learners to recognise how these particular pieces exemplify more general principles of communication. The emphasis is not on what A looked like or what happened to A when he met B or what Shelley compares the West Wind with, but on how the description of A compares with conventional descriptions of people, how the description of the meeting of A and B is to be distinguished from other ways of describing events, how the comparisons that Shelley makes contribute to the total communicative effect of the poem as a kind of discourse different from any other. A consideration of questions like these naturally brings up more general issues about the different ways in which language is used to communicate and develops an awareness in the learner which can be transferred to other instances of language use. Notice that if one looks at literary studies in this light, it is not necessary (and indeed may be undesirable) to select works on the grounds of aesthetic excellence or because they are representative of different schools and periods: the criteria for selection are pedagogic rather than aesthetic or historical and have to do with whether the works can be used to develop sensitivity to language in the most effective way. It is possible to think of a literature course which contains none of the 'classics' at all, but which nevertheless prepares the way for a meaningful encounter with them at a later stage.

In this chapter I have tried to give practical pedagogic grounds for distinguishing between literature as subject and as discipline. I have argued that literature as a subject is best defined as the study of the communicative potential of the language concerned and the manner in which this is realised in literary and conventional discourse. The subject can thus be described as an application of the stylistic approach to literature outlined in the preceding chapters. It is claimed that literary study conceived of in this way not only provides for the needs of learners whose formal education will cease in the secondary school but can also prepare others for the further study of language or literature at the tertiary level, where the subjects of language study and literature gradually approximate to the disciplines of linguistics and literary criticism. This chapter, then, has presented some of the main principles of a stylistically based approach to the study of literature. The following chapter considers how these principles can be applied in the devising of actual teaching procedures.

6

Exercises
in literary understanding

In this chapter I want to make a number of practical (if tentative) suggestions as to how the principles outlined in the previous chapter might be applied in the classroom. These suggestions are general in the sense that they are not directed at any particular teaching situation and the reader is still left with the task of adapting them to meet his individual teaching requirements. The exercises I shall propose are intended as illustrations of some of the ways the principles I have discussed might be realised: they are not intended as definitive teaching procedures.

Our principal objective is to develop in the learner* an awareness as to how literary discourse differs from conventional modes of expression. One obvious way of doing this is to set examples of literary discourse alongside examples of conventional discourse and devise exercises which lead the learner to make explicit comparisons between them. Let us see how this might be done by considering the following passage from Somerset Maugham's short story *Mackintosh* which was quoted in Chapter 4.

> He was a little man, considerably less than of middle height, and enormously stout; he had a large, fleshy face, clean-shaven, with the cheeks hanging on each side in great dew-laps, and three vast chins; his small features were all dissolved in fat; and, but for a crescent of white hair at the back of his head, he was completely bald. He reminded you of Mr. Pickwick. He was grotesque, a figure of fun, and yet, strangely enough, not without dignity. His blue eyes, behind large gold-rimmed spectacles, were shrewd and vivacious, and there was a great deal of determination in his face. He was sixty, but his native vitality triumphed over advancing years. Notwithstanding his corpulence his movements were quick, and he walked with a heavy resolute tread as though he sought to impress his weight upon the earth. He spoke in a loud, gruff voice.

* I use the term 'learner' throughout to cover both 'pupil' and 'student' in both an L1 and an L2 situation and I leave the reader to decide on how the proposals apply to particular groups of learners.

It might be said that there is not much point spending time on an examination of a passage of this kind since it is easy to understand and not particularly noteworthy as literature anyway. There are two points to be made here. Firstly, even if the learner understands the basic content of the passage and can draw sufficient information from it to answer comprehension questions relating to the descriptive detail it contains, he may still not understand its character as literary discourse. The second is a related point: although the passage might not be very remarkable for its literary quality (however this might be measured) it is an example of literary discourse and as such has certain features which are characteristic of discourse of this kind. As an isolated piece of writing, therefore, the passage is simple and not, perhaps, particularly striking. But we are not interested in it as an isolated piece of writing but as a representative instance of how literary descriptions are made. Our task is to make problematic what at first sight seems simple, to get the learner to explore the passage in order to establish principles of understanding which can then be applied to a wider range of literary discourse. The problem we wish to present to learners is not one which involves drawing as much information as possible from the passage (thereby treating it as a body of factual data) but one which involves drawing conclusions as to the nature of the description and how it differs from conventional ways of describing people. Let us consider then how the problem might be presented.

We will move towards an understanding of the literary nature of the passage by first presenting examples of conventional descriptions and posing questions which direct the learners' attention to their characteristics as discourse. The first example might take something like the following form:

PASSAGE A
  Name: Frank Ross
  Profession: Accountant
  Date of Birth: 17.4.49
  Place of Birth: Birmingham
  Height: 5' 10"
  Colour of Hair: Brown
  Colour of Eyes: Blue

The first question that might be asked on this passage is:

Question 1 Where would you find a description of this kind?

G

This will be easy for most British students to give an exact answer since they will be familiar with the standard entries in a British passport which this passage represents. Foreign learners might have more difficulty saying precisely where these particulars are to be found since even if they are familiar with passport descriptions standard in their own countries these often do not exactly correspond to those in British passports. But all learners should be able to give a more general answer by recognising that here we have the kind of description to be found on application forms and official papers of one sort or another. This first question serves a general priming function. The second directs the learner more specifically to the kind of information the passage presents and might take the following form:

Question 2 Height is given but not weight. Why?

This might appear to be a trivial question. But it has important implications. It is intended to lead the learner towards a consideration of what it is that controls the selection of detail in any particular description. Given a prompt or two, the learner can be led to recognise that the difference between height and weight is that the former is a permanent attribute of an adult human being whereas the latter is not. This being so he might then be encouraged to suppose that the reason for the inclusion of one and not the other has something to do with this difference and that height is included as a detail because the information required in a passport-type description relate to the permanent features of an individual. This prepares the way for the next question, which widens the scope of the discussion:

Question 3 What kind of information is given in this description?

It will not be difficult for the learner to discover that all the details relate to permanent characteristics (with one exception which I will come to presently). If any prompt is needed, one can ask why we have the entry

Date of Birth: 17.4.49

rather than:

Age: 25

This should yield the answer that the latter is a temporary fact (which also lacks precision) and that if it appeared in such a description one would be obliged to change passports every year or, more generally, official forms would have only a very limited period of validity. The only exception to the permanent nature of the details given is in the second entry. A person's profession is not permanent in the same way as his height, date and place of birth etc. But this piece of information (the learners can be led to conclude) is likely to remain the same during the period of the passport's validity and so it has a certain quasi-permanence: one does not change jobs from year to year in the normal run of events.

The purpose of these questions, then, is to get the learners to examine the description closely and to come to some conclusion as to what kind of information is included and why. What we are trying to do is to get the learner to realise that details are selected by reference to the purpose for which the description is made. To further this aim we might reinforce the questions already put by a question of the following kind:

Question 4 Which of the details in Passage A would you expect to find in:

    (i) An application for a driving licence

    (ii) A Health Service registration form

    Which other details would you expect to find?

Alternatively (or in addition) one could provoke discussion by a question of this form:

Question 5 In what kinds of official forms would you expect to find entries like these:

    (i) Marital status:

    (ii) Address:

    (iii) Degrees and qualifications:

    (iv) Religion:

Questions such as these are likely to cause dispute and disagreement. This is all to the good since the learners will be obliged to justify their decisions and so to examine the principles which control the selection of descriptive detail. One could then take the matter further and require them to design a questionnaire or official form for a number of specified purposes, thereby extending comprehension into composition of a simple sort. The learners should now be prepared for the next question, which relates not to the content of Passage A but to what we might call its communicative mode:

Question 6 Who do you think would write a description like that in Passage A?

This question is meant to bring out the fact that a description of this kind is composed in two stages and consists essentially in a formalisation of a set of questions and answers. In other words, it is a description of a highly controlled kind in which the person who requires the information (the questioner) specifies exactly what information he wants, and the person providing the facts, therefore, has a selection of detail imposed upon him. It might be noted in passing that what is interesting from the language teaching point of view is that here we have an example of guided composition which is at the same time a genuine use of language.

The point of these questions then is to draw the learner's attention to what is involved in writing a description, to make them aware of the nature of Passage A as a kind of discourse. The next stage presents another conventional description of a different type with which the first passage can be compared. For example:

PASSAGE B

He was about six feet tall, thin, and about thirty-five to forty years old. He had grey eyes and his hair was fair and curly. He was wearing a dark blue overcoat.

The same sort of questions can be asked as before:

Question 1 Where would you expect to find a description of this kind?

Question 2 What kind of information is given in this passage?

Question 3 Who do you think would give a description of this kind?

These questions are designed to draw out from the learner a characterisation of this passage as a type of discourse. They should, after prompting and discussion, yield these findings: A description like this one might appear as a witness's account (in a police report, for instance) and it contains information about someone's personal appearance. The information is not very precise because it has to be recalled from past impressions by a casual observer who did not expect to be required to furnish a description, but who is later asked to act as a witness. The selection of detail is controlled in this case, therefore, by the circumstances in which the description is given rather than its purpose: the information can only be that which is available from direct observation and which can be recalled later.

We can now make the analysis more precise by asking questions which make explicit the differences between Passage A and Passage B. These might take the following form:

Question 4 What kind of information appears in Passage A which does not appear in Passage B? Why?

Question 5 What kind of information appears in Passage B which does not appear in Passage A? Why?

The following conclusions might be expected to emerge. In Passage A we have details which are both permanent and personal. They are provided by the person who is being described and who is consequently both the author and the object of the description. Passage B cannot provide information of this kind since it is not available to observation by a third person. Details like date and place of birth cannot occur in a description of the Passage B type because they are not open to observation and details regarding wearing apparel are not included in Passage A type descriptions because they relate only to temporary appearance.

One might wish to reinforce these conclusions by asking the learners to move from comprehension into composition work as before. They might be required, for example, to continue the description given in Passage B or make their own descriptions from visual and/or verbal clues.

We can now present a third conventional description of a different type from the previous two and get the learners to analyse it in a similar way. For example:

PASSAGE C

Frank Ross

Mr Ross has been employed in this firm as a clerk for the past five years. I have always found him reliable and hardworking and he has the initiative to take on responsibility when required. He has a cheerful personality and gets on well with his colleagues.

We now proceed to ask the same questions as before:

Question 1 Where would you expect to find a description of this kind?

Question 2 What kind of information is given in this passage?

Question 3 Who do you think would give a description of this kind?

Question 4 How does the information given here differ from that given in Passages B and C?

With a little coaxing learners should be able to produce the following observations. This passage represents the kind of description to be found in character references. The information relates to the character of the person described and contains no detail in common with the descriptions in either Passage A or Passage B. This is not because such information is not available to the describer, who is likely to have noticed a number of physical characteristics of the person described during the period of his employment, but because such information is not relevant to the person's capacity for carrying out his professional work. Here, then, it is the purpose of the description which controls the selection of detail and in this respect Passage C has a similar function to Passage A. On the other hand, Passage C is the work of one person, and he (or she) is someone higher in authority or status than the person being described. The information given is not precise and permanent in an objective sense, as it is in Passage A, but has the character of a subjective assessment. From this point of view the accuracy of the description depends on the sound judgement of the describer rather as the accuracy of the description in Passage B depends on the perception and memory of the describer. In one respect, then, Passage C resembles Passage A and in another respect it resembles Passage B; but in most respects, of course, it resembles neither.

Now what, it might be asked, has all this to do with the understanding of literary discourse? The answer is that a close analytic study of these passages brings to the learners' notice features of conventional ways of describing which (as it has been argued in previous chapters) have to be understood as a necessary preliminary to understanding the nature of literary description, such as is exemplified by the passage from Somerset Maugham cited at the beginning of the chapter. What the learner will (one hopes) have come to recognise through an examination of these passages is that the information which is given depends on such factors as the purpose for which the description is made and on the describer's orientation or point of view in relation to the person (or other object) he is describing, whether this constrains what he can observe or the objectivity of his observation. In short, he should be able to say that a certain detail is not included in a certain conventional kind of description because it is irrelevant or because it is inaccessible to the describer, that this detail is objective and verifiable whereas that detail is subjective, and so on. With reference to the first, second and third persons in the communication situation, as discussed in Chapter 4, we can say that the learner should have been made aware that the different kinds of conventional description we have considered can be characterised by reference to the relationship between the first person describer, the second person to whom the description is directed and the third person object of description. The accessibility, exactitude and relevance of information can be accounted for in terms of these relationships.

At this point we can provide the learners with a simple scheme representing these different relationships:

III
3rd Person
Who/what is
described

I
1st Person
Describer

II
2nd Person
Who receives
the description

The describer's orientation is, of course, the relationship between I and III and the purpose of the description is the relationship between I and II. With this scheme we can now return to the three passages discussed so far and see how it can be used to characterise them. In this way we can move from an informal discovery and discussion to a more exact formulation of the learners' findings.

The kind of description represented by Passage A, for example, is compiled partly by II and partly by III. The selection of the *kind* of detail is made according to what the 2nd Person requires to know and the provision of *particular* information is made by the 3rd Person himself. So there is no separate 1st Person describer, and in consequence there is no problem in deciding on purpose since this is absolutely determined by II acting as I and no problem of orientation since this is determined by III acting as I. This might be shown as follows:

I = II	I = III
Name:	Frank Ross
Profession:	Accountant
Date of Birth:	17.4.49
Place of Birth:	Birmingham
	etc.

In Passage B, of course, the situation is very different. What I describes is controlled by his relationship with III—he may have seen him/her only once, or several times, he/she might be a complete stranger or someone quite well known. It is also controlled by what II needs to know, and in the case of a witness or someone giving evidence, II will typically subject the describer to questioning or cross-examination so as to elicit the information he wants, so the situation here is, in this respect, not unlike that in Passage A, except, of course, that here I and II are distinct. What II needs to know brings up the relationship between II and III.

The purpose of a description is to tell somebody something which he needs to know. In many cases (though not in the case of Passage A, and, for reasons just given, often not in the case of Passage B either) this involves the describer's judgement as to what is relevant and what is not. But it also involves him in a decision as to what is already known by the person to whom his description is directed: in other words, the describer, I, assesses the relationship between II and III. In the case of Passage B, II will probably know nothing at all about III and so requires the information that I gives for the purposes of identification. A person, III, exists and I has seen him: II needs details from I to enable him to identify III when *he* sees him. Potentially, then, the relationship between I and III and II and III can be the same, though operating, as it were, in a reverse direction. We might represent this in a simple diagram as follows:

PASSAGE B

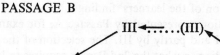

The dotted line here represents the matching procedure which leads to identification.

The diagram for Passage A will be different since essentially all that happens is that information passes from III to II directly after II has specified which information is required. We might show this as follows:

PASSAGE A

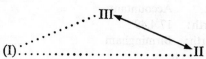

Here the dotted line indicates that I is a compound of III and II and does not exist as a separate entity.

Passage C resembles Passage B in that II can relate I's information to III. But this is not done for the purposes of identification but in order to arrive at a judgement of qualifications, suitability and so on and II will compare I's description with information deriving from other sources such as an application form (usually a Passage A type description) and his own experience of the person in interview. Another difference is that there will be no prompting from II to I as there is in Passage B. We might express these facts by removing the parenthesis around III and showing only a single arrow from I to II:

PASSAGE C

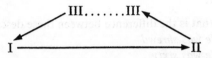

Having prepared the ground, then, we can now present the literary passage as *PASSAGE D* and proceed to investigate in what respects it differs from the others. We may begin with the same first question as before:

Question 1 Where would you expect to find a description of this kind?

Some learners will recognise the passage as literary at once, of course, though others might not. What we have to do is to get the learners to identify those features of the description which differentiate it from the others they have been considering and mark it as 'literary'. Such an identification will serve to substantiate the view of those learners who recognise that the passage is literary and to provide a means of discovering its literary character for those learners who do not. As prompt questions ancillary to the above question, we might also introduce questions like:

Question 1a Would this description be given by a witness, like the description in Passage B?

Question 1b Would this description appear in a reference, like the description in Passage C?

On the assumption that the learners will give negative answers to both of these questions, the next step is to elicit precise reasons why they think Passage D would not serve as a conventional description of the kind they have previously considered. To do this we can ask the same questions as were asked on the other passages:

Question 2 What kind of information is given in this passage?

Question 3 How does the information given in this passage differ from that given in Passage A, Passage B, Passage C?

With some learners it might be necessary to give a thorough consideration to the first of these questions before going on to the second, whereas with other learners, more readily primed by the preparation that has preceded, the two questions can be considered together. Prompt questions to support those given above might take the following form:

Question 2a What is the difference between these descriptive details:
He was shrewd
He was sixty
He was a little man

Question 3a In which of the three passages you have already examined would you expect to find details of the following kind:
He was shrewd
He was sixty
He was a little man

Question 3b Why do you think it would be strange to find the following descriptive details in the passages mentioned:
He was shrewd: in Passage A
He was sixty: in Passage B
He was a little man: in Passage C

The purpose of these, and other questions of a similar probing nature, is to direct the learners towards a precise formulation of the way Passage D differs from the conventional descriptions. Ultimately they should yield the following points. Passage D contains some details of a permanent kind such as would be found in a Passage A description (*He was sixty*, for example). It also contains details of an imprecise sort such as characterised Passage B (*He was a little man, considerably less than middle height* and not 'He was 5′ 2″ tall': (*he was*) *enormously stout* and not 'he weighed thirteen stone two pounds'). At the same time, some of the details relate to the man's character rather than his physical appearance (he is *shrewd, vivacious, resolute* and so on) and in this respect Passage D is similar to Passage

C. It would appear then that this description combines details which are conventionally kept distinct. Furthermore, it is not simply a matter of juxtaposition: the passage gives us features of the person's appearance (as in Passage B) and also features of his character (as in Passage C) but these are not kept distinct but are fused together. Thus we are not just told that he has blue eyes and that he is shrewd and vivacious but instead the features of appearance and character are described in terms of each other: *His blue eyes were shrewd and vivacious.* Similarly, we are not told that he is determined but that *he had a great deal of determination in his face.* Again, the fact that a person has a heavy tread is open to immediate observation as a physical characteristic but the fact that he is resolute requires some familiarity with his behaviour and some effort of interpretation. They are different kinds of detail, but in Passage D they are brought together into an amalgam: *he walked with a heavy resolute tread as though he sought to impress his weight upon the earth.* And then immediately after this fusion of detail we get the simple observation of the sort to be found in Passage B: *He spoke in a loud, gruff voice.*

We can now refer the learners to the simple scheme of relationships which was set up to account for the differences between the three conventional descriptions and ask: what is the relationship between the describer and the person being described on the one hand and the relationship between the describer and the person to whom he is directing his description on the other? In other words, what is the orientation and purpose of this description?

Question 4 Draw a simple diagram like those given for the previous passages to show the relationship between I, II and III in this passage.

Questions 1, 2 and 3 will have already brought out some of the peculiarities of Passage D, as pointed out above: the describer gives some details which suggest that he is an observer of the kind who might produce a description of the Passage B type, but he also gives details which are much more precise and which would normally be inaccessible to the observer—details more appropriate to a Passage A type description (and, as we shall see presently, literary descriptions sometimes provide 'facts' which are only accessible to the first person). We also find personality details of a Passage C kind blended in with appearance attributes. This mixture of information prevents one from stating what exactly the relationship is between I and III: it appears to be a combination of a number of them at a time. How can we account for this within our scheme? To answer this we have to consider the question: who is being described in Passage D? The answer is: nobody. In all the conventional descriptions that have been studied there is an external third person being referred to: a referent in the real world who can be identified and assessed, who has an appearance and a character independent of any particular account. Given a certain orientation and purpose, the three ways of describing that we have analysed can all be used in reference to any person. The same does not apply to Passage D. Here there is no specific orientation of describer to the person described, no relationship between I and III because there is no person described, no III at all. So no orientation is appropriate and all orientations are possible, not adopted for different descriptions but combined in one. The person who is presented to us in Passage D has no existence outside the passage: he is not an impression or an assessment but a creation. There is no way in which II can match what I says with the real thing: all he can do is to visualise the person on the basis of the information passed to him. The relationships between I, II and III in Passage D, therefore, can be represented as follows:

PASSAGE D

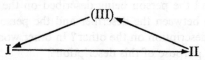

This diagram is a simple formulation of the fact that (III) is an invented person whom I and II can only identify in the imagination (and with whom both I and II can identify himself). Since the person is to be created there can be no question of the describer being constrained by any particular orientation: he may adopt the position of outside observer at one moment and describe appearance and character from that point of view, and then at another moment provide details normally only accessible to the described person himself. The distinction between I and III disappears. But notice that it does not disappear in the same way as it does in Passage A: in Passage A III becomes part of I, sharing this role with II and I does not exist as a separate person, but in Passage D it is III which does not exist. In a sense it is inappropriate to talk of description at all since to do so is to imply that there is some pre-existing person or thing to be described and in literary passages such as Passage D this is not the case.

Having linked the lack of specific orientation with the creative purpose of the passage, we can now go on to consider what other features of the description reflect this purpose. One way of doing this would be to ask the learners to do the following:

Question 5 Write brief descriptions of a conventional kind based on Passages A, B, and C using as much information given in Passage D as possible but providing more exact information when required.

This could be conducted as a class or group exercise. The following are some of the results that might emerge:

A-type description

Name: ——	(Note that these entries could be completed
	by reading further in the story from which
Profession: —	Passage D is taken)
Age:	60
Height:	5′ 3″
Weight:	13 stone 8 pounds
Colour of hair:	white
Colour of eyes:	blue

There would (and should) be discussion as to which types of information should be included and this would involve decisions as to the purpose of the description. There will also be some dispute about the exact quantitative value to give to the details *He was a little man, considerably less than middle height, and enormously stout.* This is only to be encouraged since it brings to the learners' attention precisely those factors which control the nature of a description which were discussed previously.

B-type description

He was a little man with gold-rimmed glasses, well below middle height and very fat. He had small features and blue eyes. He was clean-shaven and bald-headed except for a bit of white hair at the back of his head. He walked with a heavy tread and spoke in a loud, gruff voice. He was about sixty years old.

C-type description

There is a certain dignity in his manner. He is shrewd and vivacious in character and has a great deal of determination. In spite of his age he has a good deal of native vitality.

Again, there should have been fruitful disagreement about which details to include and this will have necessarily brought up the kind of factors which emerged from the earlier study of Passage B, and Passage C.

The next step might be to draw attention to the difference between the way information about the man's physical dimensions is presented in Passage D and the way it is presented conventionally in the A-type and B-type descriptions of the learners' own devising. To this end we might frame a question like this:

Question 6 Write down the expressions in Passage D and in your A-type and B-type descriptions which refer to the size of the person described.

This question is intended to bring to the learners' attention the way in which details in the literary passage are piled up well beyond the point required for identification, as is evident from the fact that the substance of the first third of Passage D can be contained within one short sentence in the B-type description and two entries in the A-type description. The details in the literary passage function differently: they are meant to create an impression of the person described, to make him real through words since he has no other reality. But it is not only the density of details that serves this creative function but the manner in which they are organised and expressed. We can arrange the references to size which will have appeared in the learners' answer to Question 6 in two contrasting sets:

little	enormously stout
less than middle height	large
small	great
	vast

The smallness of the man's stature and features is set in contrast with the vastness of his corpulence and this contrast creates a grotesque figure even before the writer uses that word to describe the man.

The questions that have been put so far are intended to bring out the peculiarities of Passage D by comparison with the conventional passages. A consideration of how the writer uses language to create an imaginary person, however, brings attention to bear on linguistic details in the literary passage itself. We now move from a discovery of the more general features of the discourse as a type to a scrutiny of its more particular features as an individual piece of writing. But notice that this concern with the details of how the literary description is achieved develops naturally from the characterisation of such a description as a type of discourse based on comparative procedures. It is not carried out as an isolated exercise in linguistic analysis or literary criticism. We might begin by asking a question like this:

Question 7 What is the difference between the words in Column I and the words in Column II?

I	II
small	tiny
little	minute
large	vast
	enormous
	great

The aim of this question, of course, is to draw the learners' attention to the fact that some words are unmarked for attitude (those in Column I) and can be regarded as having objective reference value whereas some are marked for attitude and convey a subjective impression (those in Column II). We can now follow up this question with one along the following lines:

Question 8 What kind of words are used to describe the man's size in this passage?

This question should yield the finding that all the words used to describe the man's height are unmarked and all those used to describe his bulk, and particularly the fatness of his face, are (with the exception of *large*) marked for attitude. It is not only, therefore, that there is greater stress on the man's fatness than on his shortness, but the former is presented in such a way as to persuade the reader to conceive of the man as the writer conceives of him: as a grotesque figure. Since there is no actual person outside the description, the reader can make no external reference and has no grounds at all for disagreeing with the image which the writer presents to him: since he can have recourse to no other source of information, he can do little else but accept the evaluation of the writer as it is expressed through his choice of marked vocabulary. Discussion of this point, essentially the relevance of the diagram produced in answer to Question 4 to the way the description is made, might be prompted by a question of something like the following sort:

Question 9 How is the selection of marked subjective words related to the absence of a real III as shown in the diagram drawn in answer to Question 4?

What we are trying to get the learners to realise is that if the person being presented in this passage is a figment of the writer's imagination there can for the reader be no clear distinction between 'facts' and 'impressions', between neutral referring expressions (like *large* and *small*) and subjectively charged evaluative expressions (like *vast* and *enormous*). In normal circumstances these expressions can be recognised as having different functions and the reader will understand them accordingly, but here they both have the same creative function. The reader has to accept them as equally valid since he has no means of validation. The grotesqueness of the man's fat face and small features which is conveyed through the writer's choice of marked vocabulary is represented as another aspect of the man like his shortness and his age. The difference between these two kinds of words is neutralised because of the relationship between I, II and III shown in the diagram, so that II has no way of assessing the relative 'truth' or 'objectivity' of one detail as opposed to another. In this discourse, *He was a little man* has the same status as (*he was*) *enormously stout* and *He was sixty* has the same status as *He was grotesque*.

This short passage from Somerset Maugham has been dealt with in some detail to illustrate how the comparative approach proposed in the preceding chapter can be used to develop in the learner not only an awareness of the nature of literary writing as a type of discourse but also, as a necessary consequence, an awareness of how English is used to communicative effect in other kinds of discourse. As was pointed out, once one has used 'control' passages of a conventional kind to establish the general character of literary discourse, one can then proceed to a closer scrutiny of the way language is used in individual instances of literary writing. Our attention now shifts from a consideration of how an instance of literary discourse functions as a whole as a piece of communication and how it relates to social factors (like the addresser's orientation to what he is referring to and who he is addressing) to a consideration of the smaller scale internal working of language within the piece of discourse itself. What this involves is an understanding of how linguistic elements take on particular values as they occur mutually conditioned in context.

This shift of emphasis can prepare the way for the study of poetry. So far we have been considering how the comparative principle that was stated in the previous chapter can be put into practice by contrasting prose passages. The assumption is that this approach will bring home to the learner certain ways in which literary writing functions as a mode of communicating. We can regard this as the promotion of an orientation to literary study. Once this orientation is established we can proceed to a consideration of how particular linguistic elements in a piece of writing contribute to its unique meaning. Let us suppose that we have treated a number of prose passages in the manner illustrated in this chapter, perhaps including more than one literary passage in a contrasting set, and that we have gradually increased the number of questions, which focus on the literary extracts and which draw the learner's attention to their idiosyncratic features. The next step might be to include poetic passages of a predominantly descriptive and narrative kind for comparison with conventional discourse but with a concentration on individual features of language use. This would then serve as a transition to the study of poetry which does not readily lend itself to this kind of comparative procedure since there are no conventional uses of language with which it can be usefully compared, and where the focus of attention must necessarily fall on the internal working of language within individual instances of poetic discourse.

This shift of emphasis does not entail the rejection of the comparative principle however. We move from a comparison between different instances of discourse to a comparison between the value of the constituent linguistic items of a literary passage and their signification as elements of the code. Whereas before we were concerned essentially with the question: what is it that characterises this passage as literary discourse, we are now concerned with questions like: what is the meaning of these words and these structures in this particular context and how do they contribute to the total message which the discourse as a whole conveys? The comparison is now not the 'larger-scale' one between discourse functions but the 'smaller-scale' one between the meanings normally attributed to linguistic elements and the meanings they assume in a particular literary work.

The kind of questions we want now are those which will bring to light the way the internal patterning of language in poems and prose pieces conditions the meaning of the linguistic items as part of the patterning. In Chapter 3 I pointed to a number of ways in which lexical items and syntactic structures took on particular values in this manner. What we need to devise are questions which will draw the learners' attention to these patterns and their communicative function. In the case of Wordsworth's *Tintern Abbey*, for example, we could get the learners to reproduce the substitution table which

H

was given as a step towards getting them to understand the notion of structural equivalence and how it can condition the meanings of linguistic elements. Again, one might get them to paraphrase poems in such a way as to break up the patterns and to compare the paraphrase with the original. There are many possibilities. As an example of one possible procedure, let us consider what questions we might frame on Frost's poem *Dust of Snow* which might guide the learner to the kind of observations that were made on this poem in Chapter 3.

DUST OF SNOW
The way a crow
Shook down on me
The dust of snow
From a hemlock tree

Has given my heart
A change of mood
And saved some part
Of a day I had rued.

What we want to do is to get the learner to recognise the association between *crow*, *dust*, *snow* and *hemlock tree*. One might begin with a question like this:

Question 1 Using a dictionary if necessary, note down as many details about the meanings of these words as possible:
crow   dust   snow   hemlock tree

The learners can be encouraged to note any detail, both those which relate to the denotation as well as those which relate to the connotation of these terms. Their findings should, in fact, provide a useful basis for a discussion of these two kinds of meaning so that the analysis of the poem can itself serve as a link between literature and language teaching, a link which, as was pointed out before, a stylistic approach to literature naturally establishes. But to return to our poem; let us suppose that the question yields (with some prompting by the teacher) results of something like the following sort:

crow:	bird—organic	ugly
	animate	noisy
	winged	bird of ill-omen
	black	
	feeder on	
	carrion—dead and	
	decomposing flesh	

dust:	inorganic	dirty
	inanimate	result of neglect
	particles of matter	
	dry remains of the dead	
snow:	inorganic	winter
	inanimate	clean
	frozen vapour	pure
	white	
	wet	
Hemlock		
tree:	tree—organic	
	inanimate	
	poisonous	

This is a very varied collection of 'details' of course (as one would expect): some have the character of semantic features, like 'organic' and 'animate'; others derive directly from dictionary citations, like 'particles of matter' and 'frozen vapour'; and others, again (those placed on the right-hand side of the page) represent different connotations of the terms under consideration. The heterogeneity does not matter particularly at this point (though some teachers might wish to guide the learners to a more refined analysis by a preliminary discussion of basic semantic notions): the important thing is that the learner has broken the lexical items into a number of component parts. The next step involves synthesis. We want the learner to discover any possible semantic links between the items by looking for similarities in the different parts. A question like the following might serve our purpose:

Question 2 Which of these terms are linked by
    (a) having the same details?
    (b) having details which are related in meaning?

The following observations are likely to emerge (given some assistance by the teacher). *Dust, snow* and *hemlock tree* are linked by virtue of the common feature of inanimacy. The last of these is linked with *crow* in that they share the common feature 'organic' without having the common feature 'animate' and *dust* and *snow* are even more closely linked in that they have two features in common: 'animate' and 'organic'. As far as 2a is concerned, then, there is no direct link between all four terms by virtue of them having the same feature(s) in common but they are brought into association through the mediation of features in *hemlock tree* which is organic like *crow* and inanimate like *dust* and *snow*, the latter two being closely linked by having two features in common (thereby, of course, making the phrase *dust of snow* easily interpretable). Notice that at this stage we are not concerned with whether or not these findings are significant for an understanding of the poem: we are simply getting the learners to recognise a semantic association, no matter how trivial it might turn out to be, with reference to certain features that they have been led to discover in their analysis of these terms.

Let us now turn to the kind of results that might come from answering 2b. *Crow* and *dust* might be said to be linked in that the dictionary entries 'dead and decomposing flesh' and 'remains of the dead' are semantically similar. One might say that there is a link, though less binding, between these terms and *hemlock tree* through the feature 'poisonous' since poison causes death. Thus these three terms are associated as having some reference to the notion of death and this notion would appear to be particularly prominent in relation to *crow* since this term also has features 'black', a colour associated with mourning, and 'bird of ill-omen'. These features are brought into prominence precisely because of their relevance to features in the other terms: in this context, 'winged' and 'noisy' are not, as it were, activated, though in other contexts of course they may be. Turning now to *snow*, it might be observed that it is possible to link this term with the others through the feature 'winter', since this might be glossed as 'the dead season of the year', and perhaps 'frozen'. Furthermore, *snow*, as has already been pointed out, shares the feature of inanimacy with *dust* and *hemlock tree*, all three terms being associated with lifelessness, and it is also linked with *crow* by virtue of rhyme. *Crow* is the only term which has the feature 'animate' as opposed to 'inanimate' but at the same time it has a preponderance of features associated with death.

We are perhaps now in a position to put the kind of question traditionally asked in literary study:

Question 3 What does the event described in the first verse suggest to the poet?

The investigation into the meanings of these four terms and the way they are linked yields evidence that what they refer to in combination, as themselves features of a composite notion, is death or lifelessness. This notion is the common factor. The kind of close scrutiny of how these terms take on value in relation to each other prepares the way for interpretation, and Question 3 can now be answered on the basis of actual evidence drawn from the analysis of the poem and not simply by reference to a general intuitive impression of what the poem is about. The event of the crow shaking snow down on him puts the poet in mind of death and we can arrive at this conclusion by recognising that a number of common elements or features of meaning in the four nouns of the first verse converge on this notion.

I am not saying that the first verse only expresses a sense of death. One could proceed further in the analysis and discover other possibilities. So far, for example, our questions have been directed at discovering common features which associate the four terms in the first verse. A question might also be asked about contrasting features: *dust* and *snow*, for example are linked by two common features, as we have seen, but at the same time they are distinguished by two contrasting features: *dust* has 'dry' whereas *snow* has 'wet' as one contrasting pair, and another set of contrasts is 'dirty' on the one hand and 'clean' and 'pure' on the other. Furthermore, although *crow* and *snow* are associated in some ways, they are also in direct contrast by virtue of the features 'black' in *crow* and 'white' in *snow*. Having provoked these observations by an appropriate question, we might then return to a reconsideration of Question 3, and we might interpret these findings by saying that what the first verse expresses is not simply a sense of mortality but a recognition that things which are distinct and which indeed may represent opposites can be reconciled by a unifying vision of an ultimate reality. So it is not just that the crow serves as a kind of *memento mori* but that its shaking down of snow on the poet's head makes him think of death and life as reconciled, just as other opposites are reconciled in the poem: animate/inanimate, organic/inorganic, dry/wet, black/white and so on. The unifying patterns in the expression of the poem represent the unifying pattern of the experience of the poet. We can conclude that it is this sense of underlying and resolving oneness that gives the heart a change of mood and 'saves' the day. The use of the term *save*, with its religious connotations, is itself significant.*

---

* Alex Rodger has pointed out to me that the syntactic structure of the poem is itself a representation of 'afterthought'. The syntax is such that the reader is led to pass lightly over the first verse in order to complete the syntactic pattern in the second. His attention is projected forward. Only when the syntactic pattern is complete to his satisfaction does the reader realise that he has missed the point of what has been said in the first verse and so his attention is then directed back to it to discover the significance of the experience which it expresses.

As another example of how the approach that has been outlined might be applied, let us consider how we might guide the learner to the kind of observations that were made on another poem considered in Chapter 4:

CHILD ON TOP OF A GREENHOUSE

The wind billowing out the seat of my britches,
My feet crackling splinters of glass and dried putty,
The half-grown chrysanthemums staring up like accusers,
Up through the streaked glass, flashing with sunlight,
A few white clouds all rushing eastward,
A line of elms plunging and tossing like horses,
And everyone, everyone pointing up and shouting.

It will be recalled that the principal point made about this poem was that it expresses a sense of dynamic movement in suspense from any particular time reference. The question that concerns us now is how we can devise exercises which will direct the learner's awareness to how this expression is achieved. We could, of course, simply point out how it is done by providing a modified version of the explanation offered in Chapter 4. But, as was suggested in the previous chapter, our purpose is not just to arrive at an understanding of this particular poem but to try and develop in the learner some kind of analytic strategy which he can apply to other instances of literary discourse. To do this we need to persuade him to participate in the discovery of meanings. We might begin by asking the following question:

Question 1
Write out the lines of this poem as complete sentences.

This exercise, of course, requires the learner to make the verb phrases finite and so to commit himself to the specification of a tense. Most learners are likely to retain the present participle and to simply insert the appropriate simple present or past forms of 'be' to yield the following sentences:

A The wind is billowing out the seat of my britches.
   My feet are crackling splinters of glass and dried putty.
   etc.
B The wind was billowing out the seat of my britches.
   My feet were crackling splinters of glass and dried putty.
   etc.

Some learners might choose to replace the present participle with the preterite or simple present form of the lexical verb to yield:

C The wind billows out the seat of my britches.
   My feet crackles splinters of glass and dried putty.
   etc.
D The wind billowed out the seat of my britches.
   My feet crackled splinters of glass and dried putty.
   etc.

If examples of these different sentences are not produced initially, the teacher can, of course, elicit them quite easily.

What we want to do next is to get the learners to consider what effect these changes have on the meaning of the poem. As a first step, we can make appeal to their knowledge of English grammar:

Question 2

What are the differences in meaning between the sentences in A, B, C and D?

The learners should have no difficulty in recalling their grammatical catechism to point out that the A and B sentences express activity extending over a period of time either in the past or including the present, that the C and D sentences express single or repeated actions in the past or present, and so on. This question serves to remind the learners of what they know about English tense and aspect and at the same time to prime them for the next question, which is intended to draw their attention to the relevance of this knowledge to an understanding of the poem:

Question 3

Which kind of sentence (A, B, C or D) is closest in meaning to the lines of the poem to which they are related?

This question is intended to arouse dispute and so to centre attention on the implications of the absence of tense in the poem. The likelihood is that there will be general agreement that the A and B sentences are closer approximations than C and D on the grounds that the latter alter an existing form whereas the others simply add something to the form to make it more explicit. But then, of course, the question arises as to which explicit form is to be preferred. The learner should now be in a position to make the kind of observations that were made in Chapter 4: that the experience is represented as dissociated from a particular time orientation, that it extends over time but is not fixed in time. The preceding questions have prepared the way, then, for a question of a more traditional literary kind:

Question 4

What kind of experience does the poem express?

The scope of this last question is restricted by the fact that it follows on from the three which precede it: it is understood that the answer will derive from the findings of the other exercises. But on its own, Question 4 would require a fuller answer than we have so far prepared the learner to provide. There is more to the experience which the poem expresses than is captured by saying that it is in suspense from time reference. Let us then extend our analysis and explore the meaning of the poem a little further.

The lack of connection between the events in the poem and any specific time-bound reality outside it is matched by a lack of connection between the events described in the poem itself. As was pointed out in Chapter 4, the poem consists of a series of noun phrases structurally unrelated to each other. There are, therefore, no syntactic constraints upon them and they could occur in any order. If these noun phrases are converted into sentences by the insertion of a finite verbal element (as is done in Question 1) they are thereby connected 'up with external reality, but they remain unconnected within the poem. The sentences resulting from Question 1 could occur in any order as well. This absence of structural links means that the events which are described are not arranged in any temporal sequence: they all occur at the same time and since no time is specified they all therefore occur simultaneously outside time. What in fact the poem expresses is a number of impressions or recollections (and I will return later to the question of whether they are impressions or recollections) unconnected with each other but associated because they occur together, capturing a sense of turbulent movement but at the same time unmoving, arrested at the same point by their simultaneity.

How might we direct the learner towards an awareness of these effects? As is perhaps apparent, they are not easy to describe with any degree of explicitness, and indeed we would not expect them to be since it is precisely the lack of explicitness that the poem seeks to convey. So that even if we wished to explain what the poem was about, the very terms we would be obliged to use in our explanation would necessarily misrepresent the meaning in some way. What we need to do is to prepare the reader as far as we can to be receptive to the meaning and to experience the poem for himself. The first step might be to draw his attention to the fact that the sequence of lines in the poem is not determined by syntactic considerations (nor indeed, it should be noted, by any rhyme scheme). The following question might serve this purpose:

Question 5

Change the order of the lines in the poem in as many ways as you can.

This exercise should reveal to the learner that although there are signals that indicate that line four follows line three and that line seven appears as the last of the sequence, the other lines of the poem are freely interchangeable. Question 5, then, might be expected to yield versions like the following:

> The half-grown chrysanthemums staring up like accusers,
> Up through the streaked glass, flashing with sunlight,
> A few white clouds all rushing eastward,
> A line of elms plunging and tossing like horses,
> The wind billowing out the seat of my britches,
> My feet crackling splinters of glass and dried putty,
> And everyone, everyone pointing up and shouting.

> My feet crackling splinters of glass and dried putty,
> The half-grown chrysanthemums staring up like accusers,
> Up through the streaked glass, flashing with sunlight,
> The wind billowing out the seat of my britches,
> A line of elms plunging and tossing like horses,
> A few white clouds all rushing eastward,
> And everyone, everyone pointing up and shouting.

Other versions are of course possible. The next step is to get the learners to think about the possible effects of these variations and this might be done by asking a question like:

Question 6

How do the changes in the order of the lines change the meaning of the poem?

Alternatively, we might frame the question in this way:

Question 6a

Do you think that the sequence of lines in the poem is preferable to the sequence in your versions? If so, why?

These questions are intended to provoke disagreement and to get the learners to look closely for any possible justification for arranging the lines in one order rather than another. It might be suggested by someone, for example, that it is appropriate for lines 3 + 4 to follow line 2 because of the common reference to 'glass'. But then someone else (perhaps the teacher) might point out that a similar consideration would require line 1 to go with lines 5 and 6 since all three refer to the effect of the wind, or that lines 3 + 4 and 6 should go together because they refer to growing things (chrysanthemums and elms). The discussion should (with the teacher's guidance!) turn out to be inconclusive on the question of preferred order and the learners will be led to realise that there is no apparent significance in the sequence of the lines.

At this point, their attention might profitably be drawn to the absence of rhyme in the poem:

Question 7

Why is there no rhyme scheme for this poem?

The point of this question, following as it does from a discussion on the lack of cohesive links between the lines of the poem, is to get the learners to realise that the absence of rhyme, which inevitably establishes a link between lines, is consistent with the other features of the poem that have been discussed. As a last stage in our return to a reconsideration of Question 4 we can now ask a question of something like the following kind:

Question 8

Why are the lines of the poem interchangeable?

It is suggested that the learners will be sufficiently prepared to be able to recognise that the poem represents a series of unordered impressions of things happening simultaneously in suspense from real time, that these impressions are associated as the similarity of the syntactic pattern of the noun phrases suggests (noun phrase + present participle), incomplete in that they are not registered by complete sentences. What kind of experience does the poem express then? A recollection of a happening in the past which by being recollected is continuously present, both past and present, outside time, fixed in the form of the poem itself.

But why a recollection of the past and not an impression of the present? This is a question which is worth pursuing since it relates to the problem of identifying the addresser and addressee in literary writing, a problem discussed at some length in Chapter 4 and taken up again earlier in this chapter in relation to the question of orientation. This poem of Roethke's contains a 1st person reference (*my* britches, *my* feet). What is the identity of this first person? Who is supposed to be the addresser in the poem? We will resume a pedagogic role and try to work out a way of bringing learners to the threshold of an answer to this question.

The first point to be made clear is the one that was stressed in Chapter 4: that the 1st person pronoun is not to be automatically identified with the poet. The most obvious way of bringing this home is to present learners with a number of literary extracts in which it is clearly not possible to make this identification of sender/addresser. Assuming that this point is understood and that it is realised that the first person addresser is not given but must be inferred, learners will readily accept that in this case there are two possibilities. The title makes it clear that the addresser is a child. But who is the child? And what is his relationship to the poet as sender? On the one hand, the poet might be expressing the thoughts and perceptions of a child as that child actually experiences them, perched on top of the greenhouse. In this case, the child as addresser and the poet as sender are quite distinct. On the other hand, the child could be the poet himself in his boyhood and in this case what is expressed is a recollected experience.

The only evidence we have that the addresser is a child is in the title of the poem. This title, with its lack of an article in the noun phrase (*Child*, not *A child* or *The child*) takes the form which is customarily associated with paintings. We can bring this to the attention of learners by asking this kind of question:

Question 9

Where would you expect to find expressions like the following:

> Women on the beach
> Girls under trees
> Man with pipe
> Nude at the fireplace

> Plum tree branch on a green background
> Child on top of a greenhouse

There should be no difficulty, given a certain amount of eliciting on the part of the teacher, in getting the learners to agree that these expressions would appropriately function (and with the obvious exception of the last they in fact all do function) as titles to paintings. Does it not seem reasonable to suppose, we might then ask, that the poem is being represented as the verbal equivalent of a painting? If this is so, then what is being represented cannot be the experience of a child imagined as taking place in the present but the experience of a child recorded as having taken place in the past. The poet assuming the role of painter cannot choose but to adopt the role of addresser, and since it is a child's experience which is expressed, it cannot but be the experience of the poet's own childhood. And it is through its very expression in the form of art (painting or poem) that this moment's experience is perpetuated, lifted out of the context of real time.

The exercises that have been proposed for this poem are meant to bring the learner to the point where he will be able to come to conclusions of this kind (though not necessarily these particular conclusions) on the basis of an actual examination of the poem. The exercises themselves may at times leave something to be desired and it may be that at times I have been too sanguine in my assessment of the effect of a particular exercise. What they are intended to do, however, is to make the learner see that the essential meaning of this poem lies not in what is described, and what could therefore be described differently without much loss through explanation, but what is expressed through a particular selection and arrangement of linguistic forms of which there can be no alternative version.

I should make it clear that I am not claiming that the kind of investigation that I have been proposing yields a definitive interpretation of poems. It is of the nature of poetry to be ambiguous and no one interpretation can capture the meaning of a poem in its entirety. What I would claim for the approach that is demonstrated here is that it provides learners with a way into an understanding of poetry and enables them to base interpretation on definite evidence whose discovery they can actively participate in. At the same time of course they are learning about the English language and the way in which it operates in use and this is likely to develop a more general ability to deal with English discourse.

Gradually, the kind of procedures I have illustrated here may become less explicitly practised as the learner develops a sensitivity to how linguistic elements take on particular values in different contexts. The point is that the procedures provide a means whereby a more intuitive understanding can be cultivated.

As I said at the beginning of this chapter, I am not trying to specify a precise set of procedures for the teaching of literature. My aim is to suggest a number of exercises that might be devised to draw the learners' attention to how English is used to communicative effect in literary writing. Formulation of the particular questions that I have presented in this chapter could no doubt be improved upon and many more questions could be devised to guide the learner to an investigation of the other peculiarities of literary discourse that were pointed out in the first part of the book. But perhaps this illustration of how the approach that has been proposed might be worked out in practice (sparse though this illustration is) will give some indication of what potential the approach has and will provoke the reader to consider how this potential might be more effectively realised in his particular teaching situation.

Stylistic analysis
and literary appreciation

It has been stressed throughout this book that the approach that has been outlined is meant to serve an essentially pedagogic purpose: to develop in learners an awareness of how literature functions as discourse and so to give them some access to the means of interpretation. It should be noted that the claim is not that stylistic analysis can replace literary criticism but that it can prepare the way for it to operate more effectively. The value of stylistic analysis is that it can provide the means whereby the learner can relate a piece of literary writing with his own experience of language and so extend that experience. The establishment of such a relationship can then serve as a base from which literary criticism, or rather a teaching approach deriving from it, can conduct its operations. Seen in this light, the kind of approach presented in this book is (in most teaching situations at least) a necessary stage on the way to literary appreciation. But this does not mean that it is sufficient as a means of expressing the full range of response which a particular work of literature might stimulate.

As has (I hope) emerged from the previous chapters, the meanings which literature conveys are of their nature elusive of precise description. There must be a point, therefore, when a consideration of the linguistic features of a piece of literary discourse shades off into an intuitive sense of significance. It would seem reasonable to suggest that there is also a point in the learner's progress when allowance should be made for the exercise of intuition and for the appreciation of the artistic value of the message which the literary work conveys. It is in the stimulation of such perception and judgement that literary criticism at its best excels. And the literary critic as teacher can with justification point out that it would be undesirable to suppress the imaginative response of learners in the interest of painstaking linguistic exactitude for its own sake. At the same time, as has been argued in this book, it would also be undesirable to allow the learner licence to indulge in any caprice of interpretation, or to adopt the less capricious interpretation of others, without a careful consideration of the supporting linguistic evidence. A central problem in the teaching of anything is to know how to exert control without stifling initiative. The problem in the teaching of literature is to know when and to what extent the learner can be allowed to proceed to the appreciation and evaluation of the broader aesthetic significance of literary works without running the risk of involvement in confusion or the traffic of ready-made critical judgements.

As was pointed out in Chapter 1, stylistics occupies the middle ground between linguistics and literary criticism and its function is to mediate between the two. In this role, its concerns necessarily overlap with those of the two disciplines. It is for this reason that stylistic analysis shades imperceptibly into literary appreciation: if it did not it would not fulfil the pedagogic purpose that I have claimed for it. To illustrate this, let us consider an example of the kind of analysis which the exercises in the preceding chapter might prepare a learner to produce at a more advanced stage of study.

STOPPING BY WOODS ON A SNOWY EVENING

Whose woods these are I think I know.
His house is in the village though;
He will not see me stopping here
To watch his woods fill up with snow.

My little horse must think it queer
To stop without a farmhouse near
Between the woods and frozen lake
The darkest evening of the year.

He gives his harness bells a shake
To ask if there is some mistake.
The only other sound's the sweep
Of easy wind and downy flake.

The woods are lovely, dark, and deep,
But I have promises to keep,
And miles to go before I sleep,
And miles to go before I sleep.

Perhaps the first thing that one notices, if one is looking at the language of the poem without troubling about what it is attempting to convey, is the preponderance of pronominal forms in the first verse. *I* occurs twice in the first line, and *his* occurs twice as well: once in line 2 and once in line 4. In addition, we have *he* and *me* occurring in line 3. There may, of course, be nothing in the least significant about these elementary observations, but we may take them as a beginning and see where they lead us.

Let us now speculate that the third person is associated with the notion of possession, basing our speculation on the slender evidence of the double occurrence of *his*. With this in mind, the next thing we might notice is that the idea of possession is given prominence at the very beginning of the poem, in that the phrase *Whose woods* is placed in thematic position. That is to say, it has been moved from its normal place in the word-order of the sentence and put in initial position where it acquires the status of the theme of the sentence. This observation might lead us to surmise that the theme of the poem as a whole has something to do with possession as well as something to do with woods.

We may now turn to consider the two occurrences of *his*. Its first occurrence is in the phrase *his house*, and its second in the phrase *his woods*. We notice that in each of their two appearances in the first verse, the woods are represented as being possessed. Furthermore, since *house* and *woods* are both associated with *his* in the parallel phrases in which they occur, we might look into the possibility of their being represented as having some kind of semantic equivalence. Since *his* only occurs in the two phrases *his house* and *his woods*, there does seem to be an implication that houses and woods are conceived of as being the same kind of thing, and that the woods are possessed in the same way as the house is possessed.

Let us explore this possibility further. The lexical item *house* may be distinguished from the lexical item *wood* in that its semantic specification in the code of the language would include the feature /+artefact/, whereas the specification for *wood* would not. The two items are not therefore semantically equivalent in the language code. If they are to be taken as semantically equivalent in the context of this poem, either *house* must lose its feature /+artefact/ or *wood* must acquire it. At this point, we might turn our attention to the rather striking verb *fill up* in line 4.

Fill up would be specified in the code as being associated with artefacts rather than with natural objects. That is to say, we would normally think of glasses, bottles, petrol tanks as filling up, rather than woods. The oddity of the phrase: *To watch his woods fill up with snow* arises because *wood* does not have the features /+artefact/ and /+receptacle/ as items like *bottle* and *petrol tank* do. It acquires these features in this context. Thus, of the two possibilities mentioned above, the evidence would seem to suggest that the woods are being represented as artefacts, and possessed in the same way as houses are possessed.

Possession bestows right of ownership. We are perhaps now in a position to suggest why it is that the first thing which is expressed in the poem is a sense of trespass. The first verse expresses the poet's feeling that he has no right to stop because somebody else has already acquired total rights over the woods by virtue of possession. They have thereby become part of the human world of rights and obligations which the poet as a member of society is bound by, so that even to stop and look at the woods is to infringe some social law of private ownership.

We may now turn to the second and third verses. Here, we notice, the woods are no longer represented as pieces of real estate: *his woods* become *the woods* and artefacts and items of rightful property become aspects of nature. But the theme of possession as being associated with human values and institutions is continued. The possessive, this time related to the first person, recurs in *my little horse*. The horse is shown to be very much a part of the world of human values. Not only is he possessed but he also possesses: *his harness bells*. Furthermore, whereas the item *horse* has in the code the feature /−human/, in the context of the poem it acquires the feature of humanness. The horse is represented as reacting like a human being: he does not understand why he should be made to stop where there is no human habitation, and where, therefore, there can be no justification for stopping in terms of any normal social requirement.

The sound of the harness bells, which might be said to suggest the world of human affairs, is contrasted with the sound of the wind in verse 3. Whereas the sound of the bells is caused by a sense of human values, that of the wind represents a freedom from the constraints which such values impose: the wind is *easy* in the sense that term has in the expression 'free and easy'. Furthermore, the fact that the two phrases *easy wind* and *downy flake* occur in combination and are structurally and rhythmically alike suggests that the adjectives are intended to be understood as referring to the same kind of quality. That is to say, the implication seems to be that it is of the nature of wind to be easy in the same way as it is of the nature of snowflakes to be downy: these are intrinsic properties in each case. We might say, then, that in the second and third verses, the woods, the wind and the falling snow are seen as symbolising a natural freedom from constraint, a world apart from that which is circumscribed by a human system of rights and obligations.

At the beginning of the last verse, the word *woods* appears again as the theme of the sentence in which it occurs. This time, however, it is both theme and subject in a simple attributive sentence. The effect of this is to provide the woods with an independent reality, having values which are not attached to them by virtue of being possessed, but which are intrinsic properties: just as the wind is naturally easy, so the woods are naturally lovely, dark, and deep. These qualities are contrasted with human values as the theme of possession is restated. Whereas, however, possession in the first verse is associated with rights, in the last verse it is associated with obligations. The use of the verb *have* is interesting here. As a lexical verb, *have* carries the meaning of possession, but as modal auxiliary (in expressions like *I have to go*, for example) it carries the meaning of obligation. In the expression *I have promises to keep*, these two senses of *have* are compounded. This might be shown as follows:

I have promises
I have to keep promises   } I have promises to keep

One might say that what is being suggested here is that the first person in the poem has promises in the same sense as the third person has woods, but the possession of promises does not bestow rights, it imposes obligations.

Finally, we might notice that the connection between the first and second lines is elliptical and is open to two interpretations. The lines, are, I think, generally understood to mean something like the following:

The woods are lovely, dark and deep but (I cannot stay to enjoy them any longer because) I have promises to keep.

If, however, one takes it that the woods, together with the wind and the snow, represent a kind of elemental freedom from the kind of constraint which controls human lives, then one might think of these lines as having something like the following meaning:

The woods are lovely, dark and deep (and represent as such a reality of elemental freedom) but (my reality must be that of social constraints and this is represented by the fact that) I have promises to keep.

Only in sleep is there freedom from responsibility.

What I have attempted to do in this analysis is to show how linguistic clues can lead to interpretation. I do not claim any special objective status for the interpretation which I have suggested, but only that it gives a definite shape to my own intuitive sense of what the poem is about. However, it is worth pointing out perhaps that the theme which this interpretation brings out: that of the reality of social constraints, of rights and obligations, in opposition to that of natural freedom, is one which often occurs in Frost's poetry (most strikingly, perhaps, in 'Mending Wall').

Here we have an interpretation of Frost's poem based on the careful consideration of certain linguistic features in it and the manner in which they relate to each other within the discourse to achieve a communicative effect. But only those linguistic features which appear to be significant have been dealt with, of course, and this means that the interpretation will not satisfy those who give prominence to different linguistic features in the poem. When the analysis which I have presented here appeared in the form of an article* it was in fact objected that it had failed to capture the central point of the poem. The following is the objection in full and my response to it:

> Reading H. G. Widdowson's analysis of Robert Frost's poem 'Stopping by Woods on a Snowy Evening' (*The Use of English*, 24, 1), I cannot help wondering whether the lines of his approach were themselves the reason why he found so much less in the poem than other readers with whom I have discussed it—namely my students. It is, I think, the case that his 'stylistic analysis' is only concerned with those features of the language which it shares with prose. There are two prominent features characteristic of verse, which he totally ignores, namely the repetition of the last line—which makes the reader think twice about what it means—and the inversion of the usual word order in the opening line, which, on re-reading, confirms the intention suggested by the last line, that it is impossible to respond fully to the poem without knowing *whose* woods indeed these are.
>
> When the reader thinks twice about what the last line means, he realises there must be a latent meaning beneath the manifest one. This reveals itself as a metaphor—'a long way to go before I die'. On re-reading, one now registers the attractive woods as the Forest of Death, and additional meaning attaches to every line. The poem as a whole rejects death without denying its appeal. Death's House is, of course, the graveyard.
>
> I am not of course suggesting that the repetition of a line or the inversion of usual word order always guides one's attention in the same way. It would perhaps be a useful exercise in stylistics to list some of the different ways in which these features do direct one's

* *The Use of English*, Vol. 24, No. 1, Chatto & Windus.

attention, and to explore the conditions which cause them to operate in one manner and sometimes in another.

(Sydney Bolt in *The Use of English*, Vol. 24, No. 3, Chatto & Windus.)

As I said in my paper, I do not claim any special objective status for my interpretation. I certainly would not wish to deny that other interpretations are possible. In the last analysis the inherent ambiguity of poetic expression is unresolvable since resolving it is bound to reduce different dimensions of meaning to one, and the recasting of a unique message into a conventional mode of communication which must of necessity misrepresent it. Ultimately, the poetic message cannot be represented in any but its own terms, and this means that no matter how exhaustive an analysis is made, it can never exhaust all possible meanings.

I take it, however, that Mr Bolt would agree with me that whatever it is that the woods represent, the poet recognises that he has obligations which prevent his yielding to it. He would agree too, I think, that the repeated last line expresses how wearisome these obligations are. But Mr Bolt feels that the repetition also suggests that the sleep referred to must be the sleep of death, and therefore that the woods must be the Forest of Death, and that the house in the village must be the village graveyard. My own feeling is that this is altogether too weighty a construction to place on this single repetition, and so I see no warrant in the actual text for his interpretation.

In saying this I do not wish to question the value of Mr Bolt's intuitive sense of what the poem is about, and there seems to me to be no point at all in arguing about the essentially aesthetic issue of the relative validity of alternative interpretations based on intuition. What one can argue about is the methodological issue of how one might guide students towards some kind of strategy for interpretation. The purpose of my paper was not to provide a definitive analysis of Frost's poem, which would have been an impossible task, but to exemplify an approach to analysis which focuses on the way language is patterned to create a message form which characterises the poem as a unique act of communication. It is my belief that such an approach can guide people whose intuitions do not respond readily to direct appeal to an understanding of how poets manipulate language to make their own meanings.

So I would not want to question Mr Bolt's interpretation of the poem; but what I would want to question is the implication in his second paragraph that this interpretation is easily accessible. He says that the 'reader' realises that there is a latent meaning underlying the repeated last line, and that this meaning 'reveals itself' as a metaphor, and that in consequence, 'one' now sees additional meanings in every line of the poem. But who is that reader and who is included in 'one'? I find it difficult to imagine school-children or students arriving at these conclusions on their own. Mr Bolt mentions his own students, and one would like to know what kind of students they are, and if it really *was* the case that they realised these underlying meanings, that the last line revealed itself to them as a metaphor, and whether, in short, they themselves arrived at the interpretation that Mr Bolt, presumably, proposes on their behalf. If, on the other hand, they were *guided* to these conclusions, as seems more likely, what kind of guidance were they given? This is the crucial question. It has to do not with whether a literary or a linguistics approach to style study yields the more satisfactory exegesis, but with what pedagogic potential they have for the teaching of literature. *

The point then is that there is not, nor can be without mis-representation, one definitive interpretation of the poem. Different readers will bring their own preconceptions and values to bear on their reading of it and will associate the poem with their own experience of reality, thus in effect creating their own connotations. I do not think that in the last analysis there is any sure procedure of evaluating interpretations in terms of their relative 'correctness'. There will, of course, be certain points of unanimity arising from an understanding of the main propositions expressed in the poem: it would be simply perverse, for example, for someone proficient in English to suggest that the poem expresses an experience of a summer morning in a city street. There will also be general agreement about what the poem communicates at the discourse level: that it expresses a longing to perpetuate the sense of peace in a moment of time and a realisation that this is not possible. But then the scope for variation of response begins to widen. Some readers will perceive a symbolic association of sleep with death and in consequence read an added symbolic value into other parts of the poem. I referred to 'Mending Wall' to support my interpretation and it has to be acknowledged that those readers who do link sleep with death in their understanding of the poem can also cite another of Frost's poems to lend support to their view. This poem is 'After apple-picking' and its concluding lines run as follows:

> One can see what will trouble
> This sleep of mine, whatever sleep it is.
> Were he not gone,
> The woodchuck could say whether it's like his
> Long sleep, as I describe its coming on,
> Or just some human sleep.

There seems to be no way of deciding impartially on the evidence of the poem itself whether 'Stopping by woods on a snowy evening' is about just some human sleep with its release from responsibility

* *The Use of English*, Vol. 24, No. 4, Chatto & Windus.

or the last long winter sleep when the moment of peace extends for ever, or, in accordance with the literary practice of expressing several meanings simultaneously, both at the same time. Of its nature, the poem provokes alternative responses which cannot be reconciled in a single interpretation. The important thing to note, however, is that the learner has to be brought to the point where he is capable of teasing out meanings for himself and where such alternative interpretations represent his own informed response. The argument in this book is that stylistic analysis can bring him to that point by developing a reading strategy for literature.

But even if the teacher of literature can see little or no value in the particular approach to literary study that has been suggested here, I hope that at least it might lead him to re-assess the role of literature in the teaching of language. There are many people who question the relevance of literature to the practical concerns of language teaching, many who regard it as an unnecessary indulgence. There are others of less practical bent who wish to dissociate it from language study in order to preserve it like a sacred relic possessing mysterious potency. It seems to me that we urgently need an attitude to literature, and a teaching approach based upon it, which, while acknowledging that literature is strange and mysterious and an object of reverence, also recognises that it is a use of language and so comparable with other uses of language; and that it is only one of the strange and mysterious ways in which human beings manage to communicate with each other.

Further reading on stylistics

Introductions:

CHAPMAN, R. *Linguistics and literature*, Edward Arnold, 1973
A short discussion of how linguistic theory and description can be applied to a consideration of peculiarities of literary style. A number of interesting issues are raised but they occur rather randomly and the book as a whole lacks coherence. Useful notes on further reading are appended at the end of each chapter.

TURNER, G. W. *Stylistics*, Penguin Books, 1973
A longer and more readable treatment of the same theme, but this book also relates the study of literary style to the more general study of language variation in use and deals in some detail with context, register and social functions of language.

Both of these books are rather discursive in presentation and neither gives a very precise idea of how linguistics can be meaningfully applied to literary writing. Their chief merit is that they provide a linguistic perspective on the study of literature. Much more precise is:

LEECH, GEOFFREY N. *A linguistic guide to English poetry*, Longman, 1969
This is a very careful examination of different features of poetic style which can be given more exact definition by reference to linguistic notions. It is essentially a descriptive book and makes no controversial claims about the relevance of linguistics to literary interpretation. Each chapter provides examples for discussion and there is an excellent set of suggestions for further reading at the end of the book.

Collections of papers:

There are several collections of papers dealing with theoretical and descriptive problems in stylistic analysis. Among them:

FREEMAN, DONALD C. (ed.) *Linguistics and literary style*, Holt, Rinehart & Winston, 1970
From the linguistics point of view this is perhaps the most comprehensive and least demanding of these collections. It is intended as a student textbook and it represents a range of different approaches. It includes both theoretical papers and examples of particular pieces of stylistic analysis. This book might serve as the transition from the introductions mentioned above to a more detailed study of linguistic stylistics.

CHATMAN, SEYMOUR and LEVIN, SAMUEL R. (eds) *Essays on the language of literature*, Houghton Mifflin, 1967
Whereas the previously mentioned collection contains papers written almost entirely by linguists, this collection also represents writers who approach the study of literary style from the literary point of view.

CHATMAN, SEYMOUR *Literary style: a symposium*, Oxford University Press, 1971
This is the record of an international symposium on literary style and the emphasis tends to be on theory rather than practice. It makes greater demands on the reader than do the collections mentioned previously.
As I said in the first chapter of this book, I have deliberately avoided the controversy between linguists and literary scholars about the relevance of linguistics to literary criticism. Readers who wish to know more about the controversy should refer to:

FOWLER, R. *The Languages of literature*, Routledge & Kegan Paul, 1971

Stylistics and the teaching of literature:

There is not a great deal of material available on the application of stylistics to the problems of literature teaching. Mention might be made of the following, however:

DOUGHTY, P. S. *Linguistics and the teaching of literature*, Nuffield Programme in Linguistics and English Teaching, Paper 5. Longman, 1968
This is a short, sound, if sometimes rather pedestrian, book intended for the teacher of English in a first language situation.

RODGER, ALEXANDER 'Linguistics and the teaching of literature' in Fraser, H. and O'Donnell, W. R. (eds), *Applied linguistics and the teaching of English*, Longman, 1969
Again, primarily aimed at the teacher in a first language situation, but this cogently argued essay has a good deal to say about general pedagogic principles relating to the teaching of literature.

WIDDOWSON, H. G. 'Stylistics' in Corder, S. Pit and Allen, J. P. B. (eds), *The Edinburgh course in applied linguistics*, Oxford University Press, 1974
This essay presents a general approach to stylistics, and illustrates it with sample analyses. It also includes a summary of a number of other approaches and provides a set of exercises.

Index

addresser/addressee, 47ff, 62, 67, 92ff, 113–114
ambiguity, 70, 114, 116, 122
anaphoric reference, 8ff, 64–66
Auden, W. H., 13, 18

Beowulf, 79
Bolt, S., 122–123
Browning, R., 18, 31
Byron, Lord, 64, 65

cataphoric reference, 8ff, 13, 65–66
category rules, 15–16, 25, 29
Chaucer, G., 79
Chomsky, N., 14
code *v* context, 27, 29, 31, 37, 46, 57–58, 63, 83
collocation, 18, 44, 45
comparative procedures, 83–84, Ch 7 *passim*
comprehension and composition, 89–90, 91, 99
connotation, 104, 105, 107, 123
Conrad, J., 66, 67
conventional communication, 47ff, 57, 63–64, 67ff, 70, 80, 84
conventional description, 87ff
cummings, e e, 14–15, 29–30

Dahl, R., 66, 67
deep and surface structure, 20–21
definite article, 8ff, 65–66
deictic reference, 11–13, 64–66
denotation *v* connotation, 104
deviation, 15ff, 27ff, 37
dictionary, 104ff
discipline *v* subject, 2–4
discourse analysis, Ch 3 *passim*
discourse *v* text, 6, 33, 37–38
double structure, 58

Eliot, T. S., 18, 42–43, 60, 69
English literature overseas, 76ff
equivalence, 39ff, 60–62, 118

Faulkner, W., 65
Forster, E. M., 41
Frost, R., 38, 104ff, 117ff

grammaticalness and interpretability, 25–26, 27

Halliday, M. A. K., 7ff, 16, 25, 65
Hardy, T., 65
Hasek, J., 53
Holloway, J., 77
homophoric reference, 8ff, 65
Hopkins, G. M., 23–24
Hughes, Ted, 16, 19, 27ff, 30, 31, 37

interpretation, 13–14, 25, 29ff, 46, 54, 70, 107, 114, 116–117, 121ff
interpretative procedures, 84–85

Keats, J., 49, 58, 63

language teaching, 80ff, 104, 124
Lawrence, D. H., 43, 45–46, 50, 65, 68, 70
Leavis, F. R., 72–74, 76–78
Lewis, C. S., 75
linguistic change, 35
linguistics *v* literary criticism, 1, 3–5, 7, 13–14
literary appreciation, Ch 7 *passim*
literary communication, Ch 4 *passim*
literary criticism, 5–6
literary description, 95ff
literature as a cultural subject, 77ff

127